BIBLE AND BELIEF

Also by J. L. Houlden and published by SPCK:

Truth Untold (1991)

Bible and Belief

J. L. HOULDEN

First published in Great Britain 1991
SPCK
Holy Trinity Church
Marylebone Road
London NW1 4DU

British Library Cataloguing in Publication Data

Houlden, Leslie, *1925–*
Bible and belief.
I. Title
220

ISBN 0–281–04546–1

Typeset by J&L Composition Ltd, Filey, North Yorkshire
Printed in Great Britain by Biddles Ltd, Guildford and Kings Lynn

For
Christopher Evans
who helped to show the way

Contents

Introduction

The papers collected here were written over a decade or so independently of each other, usually in response to an invitation to lecture or to contribute to a book of essays. Nevertheless it was not difficult to see them dropping into an order that had a sort of logic about it. They fall into a number of groups and the groups slide into each other.

The first seven chapters worry at the vexed and urgent question of the place of the Bible, as currently understood (at least among those who devote most energy to its interpretation), in relation to Christian belief and to the general theological enterprise. The relationship is viewed from both sides: how does belief fare if the 'modern' Bible is taken seriously? And how is the Bible to be seen from a point of view within the Christian tradition that does not wish to leave the Bible solely to the scholars' historical and/or literary concerns?

Within this group, chapters 1 and 2 discuss a particular aspect of the major question, especially when the force of the Christian tradition is felt together with the role of the Church as the chief bearer of that tradition. The combination of constant movement, both in belief and in the role of Scripture in relation to it, with the equally constant assertion of essential unity or even unchangingness raises hard questions, theoretical and practical, about the use and value of freedom in the study of theology. There are lines to be drawn and people draw them in different places; but there is preliminary thought to be given to the matter of how to approach that drawing of lines.

Chapters 3, 4 and 5 take the central issue of the Bible's role in relation to theology to a more general level of discussion and point towards opportunities for fresh policies as well as towards problems. They express the conviction that some of our most perplexing ecclesiastico-theological issues might look very different – and be more easily resolved – if these matters were looked at in new ways that are opened up by new knowledge and by modern approaches to the Bible. Chapter 5 does not hesitate to expose basic difficulties with Christianity's unrelenting concern with its origins, especially the endemic tendency to obscure historical realities by myths of one kind or another. Chapter 6 deals with the prospects for New Testament studies in the coming years and is therefore written from a position more interior to that discipline, though its wider useful-ness is always in mind. Chapter 7 begins to move towards specific examples, but only in relation to particular texts that indicate development of belief within the New Testament itself.

The final group of chapters (8–12) develops this approach, but the examples now concern major spheres of belief and study (chapters 8 and 10) and major contemporary problems (chapters 11 and 12). The hope here is that the reader may be encouraged, by these demonstrations of a method in action, to look afresh at other problems in a similar way.

These essays are not for the most part specialized or academic in the sense of addressing the technicalities of scholarship within a single discipline: they deliberately move across disciplinary frontiers within theology. They are not 'popular' either. So they are middle- to high-brow. They are intended to interest people of some theological skill who are concerned with these nagging issues in a modern context and, while disliking propaganda, are willing to try entering into a point of view which may well be alien to them.

I am grateful to Philip Law and his colleagues at SPCK for facilitating the compilation of this book, and to those who stimulated the writing of its various elements.

Chapters 5, 9 and 11 have not appeared in publication before. The original sources of the other essays are as follows:

1. 'Frontiers of Honesty', Eric James, ed., *God's Truth*, SCM Press 1988.
2. 'The Limits of Theological Freedom', *Theology*, vol. 92/748 (July 1989).
3. 'Daring to Study the Bible', P. Eaton, ed., *The Trial of Faith*, Churchman 1988.
4. 'Trying to be a New Testament Theologian', A. E. Harvey, ed., *Alternative Approaches to New Testament Study*, SPCK 1985.
6. 'A Future for New Testament Studies', *Expository Times*, vol. 100 (1989).
7. 'The Development of Meaning', *Theology*, vol. 72/688 (July 1979).
8. 'Jesus Christ and "The Word of God"', *The Kingsman*, vol. 20 (1978).
10. 'Doctrine Sociologised', J. Butterworth, ed., *The Reality of God: Essays in Honour of T. G. A. Baker*, Worcester, Severn House, 1986.
12. 'In a Biblical Perspective', James Woodward, ed., *Embracing the Chaos*, SPCK 1990.

J. L. Houlden
February 1991

1
Frontiers of Honesty

In his Sarum Lectures for 1968–9, published as *A Variety of Catholic Modernists*,[1] Alec Vidler recounted the sad story of the Abbé Turmel who, for many years after losing faith in the doctrines of Christianity, continued to carry out the public duties of a priest, and even after his excommunication in 1930 continued to wear the soutane and to say Mass on Sundays for his housekeeper 'who would otherwise become crazed'. Vidler is inclined to see here a case not so much of intellectual conflict as of pathological bifurcation of personality. Be that as it may, in the light of the total intellectual, psychological and social context of French Catholicism at the beginning of the present century, it is plainly hard to draw an assured line between the two diagnoses, and Turmel may not unfairly stand as a symbol of a certain kind of tragic predicament.

He was the bright son of illiterate Brittany peasants, who owed his entire culture and education to the Church. The discovery, then, that (as it seemed to him) the Church taught falsehood, about the Bible in particular, placed him in the acutest of dilemmas. Simply to give up his profession as a priest and his post as a seminary professor was scarcely possible, for, in his context and at that period, this would be to forfeit his very identity; yet no recovery of faith could take place for the arguments to effect it were unavailable. Nor could the ecclesiastical system bend to give comfort in one way or another; Turmel had indeed gone beyond

1

any reasonable bounds of church membership, certainly as then conceived. If only an escape route had not been so difficult to find!

It was an extreme case. Here was a man without alternative resources. He sprang from no solid church dynasty and could fall back on no well-placed or liberal-minded contacts in the church establishment – as William Temple and Hensley Henson could when in comparable (though less severe) difficulties at much the same time.[2] He had no liberal university to cushion his fall or allow him to hold his new views with dignity – as many more recent English and German 'rebels' have had.[3] Honesty would have been a suicidal luxury for him. So he adopted a policy of dishonesty and rationalized it: the Church had deceived him for many years by its teaching – why should he not now deceive the Church?

It was then also a peculiar case. Turmel was not saying, as the leading Catholic Modernists of his day were saying: 'The traditional formulations of Christian faith and the traditional understanding of the Bible are outmoded and misleading; here is the way to formulate and understand now.' He was saying: 'I have been deceived and I am no longer a believer.' If remaining a believer is the great object, he was no longer trying to attain it. Yet who is to say whether such a one might not retain faith if new ways of perceiving and stating Christian belief were to be freely available or if authority were more patient and pliable? In more latitudinarian circumstances he might have been the kind of dissident who forsakes what those who remain believers scarcely recognize as their faith at all, or abandons faith for reasons which many believers also see as difficulties but as peripheral in their bearing on 'real faith'. Some recent defections have evoked these responses:[4] may honesty not be too demanding, too conscientious?

But to return: how far Turmel's behaviour was a

matter of his own personality and how far the effect of his circumstances may now be of purely historical interest. Bizarre as his case is, it throws into relief many features of a persistent issue in the practice of theology in relation to the Church, in a way sufficiently close to, yet sufficiently far from, present-day Western circumstances to be both instructive and stimulating. At its simplest, the issue is: how important is honesty in the Christian theologian's work? What are its terms and what is its character?

For many, both insiders and outsiders as far as faith is concerned, the thing is clear-cut. Particularly in a pluralist society with commonly recognized (if only vaguely defined) criteria of evidence and truthfulness, the Church is perceived as now a voluntary society competent to make its rules and define its membership (sometimes, as in England, with some blurred areas derived from the past). It may once have been different, but now no one compels people to join or to remain. So it seems clear: if they cannot conform, they must be outside. No one now need face the agonies of Turmel.

There is of course an immediate qualification, even when the situation is judged at the secular level of 'the Church as voluntary society': members of such bodies may properly attempt to change the rules and re-define the conditions of membership, even by means of lengthy campaigns of education and persuasion. No one, however strongly he perceives Christianity as an unchanging faith, can reasonably maintain that in all matters such adjustment is ruled out. Plainly, as a result of initiatives from all levels of the Church, top, middle and bottom, it has occured constantly in the past. Plainly too, there is an uncertain dividing line between permissible adjustment and impermissible change which does violence to the heartland of faith or (more prosily) commonsense Christian identifiability. The line may be felt to be discernible only with hindsight, and the cynical observer will say that the chief determinant of its positioning depends on whether the aspiring reformer succeeds or fails.

Such considerations affect all kinds of bodies – political parties and charitable societies as well as churches. They affect bodies possessing all kinds of ethos (open or authoritarian) and structures (democratic or hierarchical). But in the case of the Church, other factors reinforce the position of the would-be reformer who has no wish to leave the fold, notably the provisional character of all speech and formulation about God.

Religious bodies are in a strange position in this respect: the more central to faith the matter in question, the more susceptible it is to the operation of provisionality of formulation and (if the point can only be accepted) the weaker the position of the traditionalist; yet such subjects, being central, are precisely those on which, in religious bodies, the question of exclusion from membership most appropriately arises, and in relation to which awareness of the inadequacy of human talk about God is least likely to be admitted – for the very identity of the body concerned seems to be at stake.[5] That a reformer holds and seeks to commend new views on, for example, funeral procedures or the ethics of gambling, and even persists in being out of line on these matters, may seem poor grounds for raising the question of his or her integrity in relation to membership. Yet when it comes to matters which manifestly and understandably do raise that question (belief in God, understanding of the incarnation), the issue of provisionality comes firmly into view and baffles action. Experienced and 'history-wise' authorities may be reluctant to exclude the dissident who is acting with integrity – whatever the clamour from those not given to subtlety of perception or moderation of tongue.

It is of course possible (and has in the past been

usual) for church authorities to deny provisionality in the statement of belief and to insist (whether out of concern for orthodoxy or for civil order) on particular formulations as if possessing 'final' validity, but authorities thereby run serious risks: at the least, the future charge, probable on the basis of many past examples, of short-sightedness and foolishness; and more, the general depressing of credibility and the trivializing of religion that comes from enforcing belief about the transcendent encapsulated in ephemeral terms.

The matter is made worse when one knows (and these days everyone may know) the mechanisms by which churches arrive at their statements: the bureaucratic and political, rather than intellectual pressures which commonly predominate; the calibre and type of those primarily involved, often simply those willing to devote energy and able to devote time to the elaborate machinations required. It takes a lofty and penetrating conviction of the divine guidance operative in these procedures, and of its overriding authority, to compensate for this acquaintance with the earthly details – and of course this highly theological conviction is itself subject (please God) to the criterion of provisionality which is in question.

For some, nevertheless, this conviction has been the determining factor: in the 1920s Abbot Cuthbert Butler of Downside deliberately turned aside from research into Christian origins and the New Testament because of the risk of collision with ecclesiastical authority,[6] presumably not because of sheer pusillanimity and cynical evasion but because of an underlying belief that 'the Church', however improbably and unimpressively embodied for a particular purpose, had *ultimate* competence as the organ of Christian truth, even where there were matters susceptible of historical investigation and vulnerable to its uncertainties, as had now become painfully plain.

In more modern form, some such complex of attitudes seems to underlie certain areas of the work of a scholar like Raymond Brown, the American Roman Catholic writer on the New Testament whose books are so widely and deservedly appreciated. In his study of Matthew 1—2 and Luke 1—2,[7] he confronts, as he must, the implications of his historical exegetical work for the doctrine of Jesus' virginal conception. He devotes an appendix to the question and concludes that 'the *scientifically controllable* biblical evidence leaves the question of the historicity of the virginal conception unresolved' (p. 527). The italics hint that other kinds of 'evidence' must be available which are relevant to the matter, presumably (though it is not clearly said) some form of magisterial church teaching. Yet of course the setting and emergence of that teaching in what he shows to be its many and varied forms are themselves equally open to scientific control, and one is left wondering how exactly it can carry force when one recognizes that its proponents took a wholly optimistic view of historicity. Brown is left with (*a*) an *opinion* that 'it is easier to explain the New Testament evidence by positing historical basis than by positing pure theological creation' (pp. 527f.), and (*b*) a belief in the virginal conception as an 'action of God's creative power' (nevertheless 'not a phenomenon of nature' [p. 531]!) whose precise purpose seems to be elusive. Such an exercise may strike some as a determination to stay sitting on the branch while cheerfully sawing it through to breaking-point. And the purpose, or perhaps the trusted way of safety? Surely it is the conviction that in the end the magisterium *knows* in the long term if not in the short, and is anyway the sphere whereby God's purposes are spearheaded in the world.

Those who, placed outside this particular framework of theology and so this particular posture in which to discern what honesty requires, gasp at such a manner of proceeding, should reflect that some form of it may stare them in the face at any moment. Whenever, confronting the apparent need as a result of theological investigation to modify the traditional patterns of faith and so to place themselves at variance with the main stream, they nevertheless try to insist on their integrity in remaining within the fold, they may well be positing a location where their view is legitimized, even if that location is no earthly organ of the Church but the very mind of God himself.

So far this discussion has concerned largely the interaction between the nonconforming or reformist theologian and the Church; it has commented on some aspects of the issue of integrity that may arise. Where the dissident is employed by a modern Western secular academic institution, or (to raise the tone) feels the moral claim of the ethos such institutions represent, the issue may seem in effect non-existent: surely it settles itself. The difficulties arise purely when one is involved with the Church: its rules, its heritage, its inability to move in the light of translucent evidence but only by the kind of slow, mysterious adaptability, almost invisible to the naked eye, found in the evolutionary processes of nature itself.[8] It is not surprising that the examples that have sprung most readily to mind have come from Roman Catholicism, where these factors appear most sharply in the modern world. But lay all that aside, and integrity is easy; and its claims are among the most elementary moral requirements that we know. In this sense, there are situations where a church may represent a standing temptation to immorality, if only by placing institutional survival or cohesion in one form or another above ordinary truthfulness, or fostering a style of loyalty or fellowship in which the moral priority of truthfulness is blurred or underplayed (no doubt in the interests of other 'truth' whose defensibility is precisely what is in question).

All the same, the overriding character of the high-minded academic's integrity may be challenged for better cause than that given by the aspects of ecclesiastical culture just listed (in effect, the inherited tradition). Despite all discouragement, the belief that the nature and content of theological wisdom are better understood and described by committed insiders than detached outsiders has force. It is a belief which profits, be it noted, from a shift in terminology and accent: from theological *truth* to theological *wisdom*; from something which is likely to be conceptual and to lend itself to dogmatic formulation and authoritative pronouncement to something which will extend to more elusive and even tentative expression but suggests greater depth of reflection and strength for all that. While it may be more subjective, it will also be wider in scope, embracing moral and spiritual as well as intellectual dimensions and seeking to unify them within a *mode of existence*. Such wisdom is of course far from immune to self-deception and failure to face reality – indeed it is the favourite refuge of the woolly – but at its best it presents strong credentials to opposing viewpoints and is capable of making them shrivel into superficiality, a fate to which the detached outsider is peculiarly vulnerable at its hand. Such is the wisdom that can be a quality of the insider. It is of its essence to share the experience of religion, not simply to describe it. In modern circumstances, it will at its best (and with regard to this wisdom, only the best is tolerable) be able to combine commitment with detachment from all particular forms of theological formulation and religious life, seeing them as but transient approximations to the true and the good. It is then as far as possible removed from the absolute attachment to particular forms of ministry or liturgy or architecture to which religious people are prone, while at the same time it generates intense love of whatever forms seem best for the moment. It will of course face chronically the charges of instability and weakness. Precisely this sort of wisdom, with its fusion of the intellectual, the moral and the spiritual, calls into question the claims of certain styles of integrity in theology which at first sight seem beyond challenge, for example that of the independent scholar who feels responsibilities to standards and styles of truthfulness which churches, with their multifarious membership and innate caution, sense less keenly.

We may illustrate the matter by examining it in the setting of early Christianity witnessed in the New Testament. In those documents, it is doubtful whether the question of theological honesty is ever raised in the senses most recognizable to us. They are too much a product of the intellectual developments of the past two centuries and of secularization for that to be possible. There is no sign in the New Testament of people suffering a sense of conflict between a high service of truth and evidence on the one hand and authoritative teaching on the other.

But there are instances, of which Paul, at the very fount of the tradition, is much the most striking, where questions of integrity are to be found such as are not beyond our capacity to understand with sympathy bred of experience.

The most far-reaching example concerns Paul's attempt to reconcile the universal role of Jesus with his inherited conviction concerning Jewish particularism.[9] It involved the question of the Law's validity (in part or as a whole? for some, for all, or for none? in past or in present?); it involved a mental picture of Israel's history and its role in history as a whole (top dog or under dog? privileged or discarded? with a future or only a past?); and it involved a framework for understanding God's providential ordering of things (unwavering consistency or discontinuities? discernible plans or inscrutable counsels?). Here was a collection of issues which were far from being theoretical puzzles one could ponder at leisure, but were rather matters on which one's very self-understanding, the intelligibility of one's 'world', depended. For Paul, the irruption of Jesus as God's chosen envoy and his own belief in Jesus' consequentially urgent significance for everybody, rendered highly problematic all conventional and traditional assessments of that 'world'.

There have been many efforts to weld Paul's statements on these questions into a consistent whole. To succeed in the endeavour would be to vindicate the integrity of both Paul and Scripture, a prospect lending zeal to the task. A more candid and realistic examination convinces many students of Paul that the quest is misconceived. While Paul's words make an identifiable set of points, those points are evidence of a variety of tendencies, a number of different 'probes' into the thought-situation which he faced. In that sense, Paul is a man seeking integrity rather than expressing it. It is as if, seized by the single clear conviction of Jesus' unique and crucial significance, he was, in the letters before us, *in process* of reorganizing other elements of his mind's truth, his 'world', around that central belief. (Whether, in the terms available to him and as the problems then presented themselves, *any* satisfactory reorganization was possible is another matter.)

It is of course debatable where this places Paul in relation to theological honesty. Putting it crudely: does he win points for accepting new truth brilliantly clear to him, even if its implications were obscure and even confused? Or lose points for accepting new data which did not clearly cohere with truth already revealed and established? Was he admirably adventurous in letting his 'world' go, or a raiser of dust (still not settled!) which can only blind the faithful pilgrim? Then: is honesty to God a matter of acceptance of authority and authenticated tradition in belief, or is it acceptance of 'call', yielding a wisdom which may have its own kind of fused integrity at a level where belief, behaviour and prayer are one? 'Against such there is no law' (Gal. 5.23).

Another example relates to Paul's moral and pastoral counselling. It is the familiar case of idol meat,[10] whether Christians should eat meat which had, en route to the butcher and the table, been the object of pagan ritual 'treatment'. We now have a very full understanding of the circumstances surrounding this matter in the life of a Greek city and we can enter into the social realities involved for a Christian group which contained members from various levels of society. Nevertheless, the question of moral strategy on which Paul rules in 1 Cor. 8 is plain enough: shall theological truth be acted upon regardless of the irrational susceptibilities of some members of the group? An added element in this case is that in all probability it was the richer ones who discerned the key theological truth that 'idols are nothing' and the poor who had scruples, taboo feelings, about association with pagan cults. Paul firmly subordinates the claim of theological truth to that of love for the 'weaker' members. Has he not then failed in intellectual integrity, forsaken a fundamental piece of honesty, for the sake of ignoramuses? Will not such a policy, consistently pursued, result in a religion where truth counts not at all and all manner of superstition happily gets away with it? So the honest outsider may easily think. But there is an insider's wisdom ready to speak on Paul's side (though whether it should be determinative is still up for discussion). It derives from the perceiving of realities deeper still than honesty about the truth concerning God. God has called into being a community of persons in allegiance to him in the way of Jesus. It is together that they must learn to live in relation to him, and that 'living' is not chiefly a matter of articulated truths about God's nature, but of

11

conviction *experienced* in life together. There is more than one route by which truth may emerge and finally enter into understanding, more than one order in which wisdom may be acquired. If this is a way of now assessing Paul's judgement in this case, then it is hard to deny it the tribute of a valid kind of honesty. The modern Christian who wonders whether to abandon (as it seems) valued 'truth' in the interests of relations with those of other Christian traditions or of other faiths may find himself facing a not dissimilar set of considerations.

The challenges facing the Christian of the present day who wishes to combine commitment with integrity in the face of discouragement or conflict are in many ways not much like those discernible in the career of Paul. There are, however, as I have hinted, sufficient similarities to give pause to those who are apt to go for simple resolutions in one direction or another. Religious honesty is a complex quality: not synonymous with speaking one's mind in all circumstances, nor with uttering every new thought in a field where criteria of excellence are not wholly clear or easy to come by, still less with enjoying intellectual excitement; more a matter of weighing all relevant considerations, then combining firmness with tentativeness, strength with provisionality, clarity with scepticism, because of the character of our knowledge of God and our pilgrim-like relationship with him.

NOTES

1. Alec Vidler, *A Variety of Catholic Modernists* (Cambridge University Press 1970); for Turmel's career see pp. 56–62; he lived from 1859 to 1943.
2. See F. A. Iremonger, *William Temple* (Oxford University Press 1948); ch. 7; Owen Chadwick, *Hensley Henson* (Clarendon Press 1983), ch. 6.
3. The cases of Hans Küng at Tübingen, of the contributors to *The*

Myth of God Incarnate (SCM 1977), of Don Cupitt, and perhaps of John Robinson himself.
4. The cases of Michael Goulder and Anthony Kenny spring to mind.
5. These considerations have been close to the surface in numerous modern theological storms: over *Honest to God* (1963); Maurice Wiles' *The Remaking of Christian Doctrine* (SCM 1974); *The Myth of God Incarnate*, edited by John Hick (SCM 1977); and David Jenkins' utterances, leading to *The Nature of Christian Belief* (Church House Publishing 1986), a statement by the bishops of the Church of England.
6. Adrian Hastings, *A History of English Christianity 1920–1985* (Collins 1986), pp. 152f.
7. Raymond E. Brown, *The Birth of the Messiah* (Geoffrey Chapman 1977), see especially Appendix IV.
8. See my editorial in *Theology*, vol. XCI (January 1988).
9. See especially E. P. Sanders, *Paul and Palestinian Judaism* (SCM and Fortress 1977); id., *Paul, the Law and the Jewish People* (Fortress and SCM 1983); Heikki Räisänen, *Paul and the Law* (J. C. B. Mohr [Paul Siebeck], Tübingen 1983); Francis Watson, *Paul, Judaism and the Gentiles* (Cambridge University Press 1986).
10. See Gerd Theissen, *The Social Setting of Pauline Christianity* (T. & T. Clark 1982), especially ch. 3.

2
The Limits of Theological Freedom

Our question concerns the proper extent of freedom in the expression of Christian theology. It is the question which was discussed irreverently, and chiefly ecclesiastically and ethically, in David Lodge's novel, *How far can you go?* It is the question raised explosively every time a fifty-year-old but currently unfashionable idea catches the public's eye.

There is of course an intellectually trivial sense in which, in an open society, that freedom is absolute. That is, in a society open in the relevant respect, nobody will intervene to shut you up or punish you, at least overtly, if you state Christian faith in forms that are out of line with the tradition or rather the present understanding of it. There are also issues, again intellectually trivial (though in other respects not trivial at all), concerning the extent to which churches can reasonably permit speculation and deviation among their members; and the extent to which persons who, in their own eyes or those of others, speculate and deviate, should claim to be doing Christian theology. These issues, much to the fore and often treated as if they were intellectual issues, are strictly matters of discipline. They relate not to truth but to the question how far the rules of the club can appropriately stretch. Of course there is then the question whether or not these irregularities should be settled on grounds of truth (and we may hope that they may play some part) or instead on grounds of the internal politics of the institution; but again, that is not strictly an intellectual question, though it may involve an intellectual component.

Our question is about the proper constraints there may be in the matter of development or innovation in Christian theology, understood as an enquiry into truth. That is, let us suppose that one's aim is on the one hand to follow the demands of criteria of truth that become apparent from time to time, or of sheer facts which may emerge, and on the other hand to articulate Christian allegiance and Christian understanding; then what intellectual constraints, if any, apply? It seems easy enough to see how one could follow one path or the other. When it comes to combining the two objectives, then it seems necessary to raise the subject of constraints – at first sight not a happy word when freedom seems to be a primary good. It may of course be impossible to state these constraints abstractly or to predict how they may arise in hypothetical future situations – that is a not unreasonable position – but all the same, few would deny that there is a question here worth discussing.

Before facing it directly, and as a way of approaching it, we should first reflect on the Christian wisdom (and indeed other kinds of wisdom, for they interrelate) on the subject of freedom. If freedom is an aspiration which we entertain as we go about our theology, a condition of its possibility of which we are conscious once we consider the matter, then it must be worthwhile achieving some clarity about its character and its propriety. Freedom is of course a matter of the deepest ambiguity and complexity. In the West, we are all conditioned to suppose that it is a good beyond compare, an achievement behind us, requiring vigilance to retain but not work to attain, and at root an identifiable commodity even if it is often blurred in practice by human perversity.

Yet so inherently complex and even paradoxical is the concept of freedom, that from the very bases of our culture it is full of ambiguity. Aristotle's *Politics*, for instance, already contrasts two senses of the word. There is, he says, a mean and unworthy kind of freedom, the freedom to do as you like; and there is the freedom which alone is desirable, freedom to obey the laws of the city (one may say, not quite fairly, the society) in which one participates. Here are the seeds of Aquinas' distinction along similar lines between *libertas minor* and *libertas maior*: freedom *from* impediment and restraint and freedom *to* achieve one's proper and allotted end, that is, ultimately, the service and enjoyment of God.

The earliest Christian writers too worked with an essentially similar structure, again far from our easy sloganizing on the subject. In the New Testament version of the matter, the two senses correspond to two aspects of early Christian experience – the loss and the gain involved in moving into the Christian sphere. There was, on the one hand, a many-sided achieving of freedom *from* entities which were either inherently oppressive (such as sin and death) or were now perceived as oppressive (the Jewish Law and spiritual powers). On the other hand, there was submission, even slavery, to Christ; in Aristotle's terms, freedom *to* obey him. Paul makes delicate verbal play with this new freedom which is also slavery (Rom. 6.18). Already for him the word seems appropriate to hit off the very nature of the new life which he has entered, and the Gospel of John takes it up in a similar sense. There are the twin statements of the point: 'the truth will make you free' (8.32) and 'if the Son makes you free you will be free indeed' (8.36). In effect, Jesus is both the agent and the sphere of what is seen as 'freedom'. The term refers, then, to the enjoyment of a new, invigorating ethos which one has come to share, rather than to a sense of mere release from past ills. It is as if, reaching the mountain top, one rejoices in the pure air, and in one's exhilaration speaks of a freedom hitherto unknown. Primarily, it is the freedom *to* be committed to Christ and all that he signifies, or else the freedom *of* being so committed, and secondarily, it is freedom *from* an old, inferior state of affairs. With the question of one's freedom in the act of transition, one's autonomy of choice, the New Testament is minimally concerned. Rather, people are compelled, seized, drawn. However important that aspect of freedom may be for us, for those writers, not only was such an interest not much in the air of the times, it was also unlikely to arise when the new good was so manifestly desirable. When one has won on the pools, one does not pause to consider how free one was in the moment of filling in the coupon.

I have no doubt that this sense of a new framework of existence, given by God through Christ, in which one's destiny is alone fulfilled and fulfillable, is central to the Christian idea of freedom – in so far as it is possible to speak of such a thing in that unequivocal way. Here is its centre, its glory, and also, as we shall see, the seed of difficulty. It is, then, a term which has had a certain amount of currency as an equivalent of other terms: entering the Kingdom, eternal life, justification, reconciliation. All express, in different semantic or symbolic fields, the same conviction: that one's good is realized within the God-given and Christ-coloured sphere of existence. Naturally this term, like the others, has its own range of structural possibilities. We think of the most succinct statement of all, imprinted on countless minds and expounded in countless sermons, and derived straight from Pauline beginnings, the Sarum and Book of Common Prayer morning collect characterizing God – *cui servire regnare est* (whom to serve is to reign), with the English moving from 'kingdom' to 'freedom' language: 'whom to serve is perfect freedom', thus clarifying the Pauline allusion, but losing something in sheer dramatic quality.

If freedom has this range of overlapping associations, it is naturally a property shared with others, as it is also a relational term: to be free is to be in a certain standing both with God and with all those in the same sphere of commitment. Conversely, it is a possession not felt as freedom at all by someone who has not made the commitment. To find this sphere of life free rather than oppressive requires a positive act of will or desire, a vote in favour of the Christian sphere, or else a surrender to the drawing or the seizing that has come one's way.

Earlier, I spoke of freedom as an aspiration, something to be sought after. In the perspective we have now arrived at, it is more something to be enjoyed, a way of thinking of one's possession, one's framework of life. Far from being a person-centred absolute, an absence of all restraint, it depends upon an identifiable framework for its recognition and enjoyment. Putting it another way, we may say that freedom is conditional upon such an identifiable framework, and there will be as many freedoms as there are frameworks available for enjoyment.

Marxist theory has always accepted such a conceptualization with a candour that leaves the Western liberal aghast, though Thomas Hobbes of Malmesbury taught it brutally to the English long before. Freedom consists in identifying oneself with the historically determined purposes of society or the state and living accordingly. To seek a way of life across the line of those purposes is to forfeit the right to belong to society. It invites marginalization or even elimination.

The Western liberal tradition, however, for all its lip-service to individual rights, has its own less candid equivalents. John Locke's advocacy of freedom of ideas did not extend, in the crucial political sphere, to atheists or Roman Catholics: the oaths of the former could not be trusted, for they had no fear of God, the loyalty of the latter could not be relied upon, for they owed allegiance to a foreign power. While those particular limitations on freedom have vanished from our society, it is not hard to think of other pockets of opinion which are effectively denied full and free expression, just as other (and doubtless wider) ranges of opinion are denied expression in many other societies. For our purposes, the range of opinion which is effectively denied freedom in a given society is irrelevant. What matters is that in avowedly free societies, as well as in societies widely regarded as unfree, there is restriction. Freedom is conditional upon a given framework of values and institutions by which the society identifies itself. As far as most members of the society are concerned (and certainly those who profit from the society), that framework is likely to go unremarked and to be largely taken for granted. Whatever value is placed on freedom *from* restraint, freedom *to* conform to the norms of the society, norms which are relative to that particular society, is also valued and in the end prevails. Whether a given individual perceives the society in which he or she lives as free or oppressive depends, of course, wholly on the opinions they wish to hold or express or the lines of action they wish to undertake. Those whose desire for freedom extends only to the wish to have liberty to engage in bee-keeping and to express their views about it are likely to feel as free in Bulgaria as in Sweden. A person who has no desire to hold any views at variance with the current regime will feel perfectly free: he or she will be wholly fulfilled within the framework provided, whatever its character happens to be. Conversely, English people employed in the security services who wish to publish

their memoirs or complain of certain government activities will find their freedom restricted; as will an
unemployed black in Handsworth who longs for
amenities which the majority take for granted. The
given framework frustrates the fulfilment of their goals
in life and fails utterly to enhance their freedom.

If we move at length to the area of theological enquiry
as one sphere of activity within society, we find that
considerations such as we have outlined for society as a
whole apply here also, while certain additional factors
come into play. It may be objected that the move from
society to theological enquiry is illicit, in that it does not
compare like with like. The objection might be removed
if one were to compare society at large with the Church,
whether in a wide or narrow sense; but whatever may
once have been the case, theological enquiry is no
longer simply a function of the Church. It is conducted
also in secular contexts, both public and private, both
universities and homes. Yet, with whatever detachment
from the Church it may often be carried on, theological
enquiry, unless it remains in the ultimate privacy of the
individual's bosom, is nevertheless a social activity,
conducted in a community of persons, however loosely
constituted. There is a sense of common enterprise, the
attempt to elucidate and formulate discourse about
God, for our present purpose in a Christian context.
Once the matter of common enterprise is recognized,
questions of power, value and truth arise as condi-
tioning factors in the elucidation of freedom. Let us
then speak of the theological community, being content
not to define it more closely than these remarks indicate. Such a community faces, in its measure and in its
manner, all the complexities and ambiguities of freedom that have been identified. They apply at any given
moment in its existence and in its movement through
time.

As in the case of society at large, this community is

bound to operate with its own set of restraints and liberties. In any given situaton, they will be relative to the complex circumstances in which the community finds itself. These circumstances will consist of both its own internal structure and composition and its relationship with other communities, including some, such as society at large, with which it has overlapping membership and so the likelihood of a significant dialectic of assumptions, obligations and rights. The community will make its judgements – often silently – on what is or is not intellectually permissible within the bounds of its enquiry, broadly on the basis of what is perceived to be supportive or subversive of the enterprise as a whole. In the state, it may be arguable whether citizens should be free to criticize the sovereign or (let us say) the security services: but if they import an enemy's weapons into the state's territory, they will rightly be seen as subversive of the state's very existence. One way of looking at our original question is to ask whether, in the sphere of things which concerns us, anything can have the finally subversive quality which treason has in the case of the state.

I must confess to a certain unease at the direction which these reflections are taking. On the one hand, observation and common sense teach that freedom (whether it be the 'freedom *from*' or the 'freedom *to*' sort) is bound to be relative to a particular set of circumstances. It cannot be absolute if cohesion and community existence are to be maintained. No human enterprise can survive without some conditions whose absence would render it futile. In that sense, freedom can never be a primary practical demand, and it is foolish to speak of it as a human right. It will always be a matter of 'freedoms', and they wil be hedged around and defined. To some in a given situation they will seem wholly adequate, to others they will feel like oppression: it depends how far the individual is satisfied with the truthfulness or goodness of the given framework.

On the other hand, it is deeply unsatisfactory if there is no room for movement in the kind of freedom available as circumstances of various kinds change. As freedom is a relative matter, any shift of circumstance is bound to mean a change in the practical effect of existing freedom. Yet for movement to be sought, there has to be a sense of where new developments might profitably and truthfully lie. Otherwise, the claiming of freedom will be arbitrary and wilful. In the special matter of theological enquiry, we may lay down certain principles.

1. All history leads us to think that, if responsive movement (i.e. recognition of the demands of new situations) is to occur, decisions about propriety cannot be left in the hands of constituted authorities, whether churches or even universities. There may be exceptions to this bare-faced rule. Sometimes, when churches are facing severe challenge to their very integrity or existence, they may be moved to innovate in the cause of truth or virtue. We may point to some parts of Central and South America in relation to liberation theology, or some of the Anglican provinces in relation to women's ordination. In such circumstances, new kinds of freedom are available because new truth comes to be recognized. Similarly, where universities are not particularly powerful in society and do not feel heavily responsible for the stability of society, they will be more disposed to encourage or at least not suppress change, in accordance with need. But in the greater number of cases, churches in particular will be inclined to restrict freedom rather than encourage it and to maintain an idea or picture of a given set of circumstances long after the reality has changed. Even when they innovate and enlarge freedom, they will often claim to be reviving or reinterpreting what is very old.

2. The theological enterprise has the unique feature that by its very nature it can never plausibly claim finality. As its subject-matter is the transcendent God and its task the encapsulation of thought about him in shifting and fallible words, theology, more than all human enterprises, has every reason to encourage freedom and to err on the side of generosity in this respect. For who knows what ideas may turn out to be illuminating if pursued further, and helpful if given prolonged exposure to air? It is of course ironic that it is thought in precisely this area that has occasioned more human intolerance than any other! We are all experts on the unknowable. Yet every so often, the implausibility of that position, and the fragility and provisionality of theological statement break through into conscious-ness. Then, freedom will be ready to change its shape, in accordance with new requirements.

3. All the same, however great the appropriateness of generosity, it cannot be the case that in this area 'anything goes'. It would scarcely be reasonable or fitting if, in the matter of our apprehension of the most far-reaching questions of our self-understanding, we should be wholly undiscriminating, and toss ideas around with the lightness associated with the bar par-lour or the sherry party. We may no longer quite think that eternal salvation depends on orthodoxy of belief, or even be sure what 'eternal salvation' precisely means, but it would be strange to suppose that all religious ideas are equally valuable merely because they are held. Religious 'dottiness' is not a meaningless concept.

4. The most helpful way forward may lie in a pro-found acceptance of two features of the pursuit which concerns us. In a way, they amount to the beginnings of a programme.
(a) The first is a giving of genuine primacy to the transcendence of God and therefore to the impossibility

of final statement concerning him. It is not that this principle is not affirmed: it is simply not acted upon rigorously. Give a theologian less than half a chance, and his or her next words implicitly deny it.

(b) The second is a recognition of the character of theological exploration as less the acquiring of a knowledge and more the acquiring of a skill, an ability to feel at ease with a limitless array of resources which neither dictate one's own thinking nor free one from the responsibility of undertaking it. There is of course no way in which such an approach to theological exploration in a context of basic commitment, whether within the churches or elsewhere, can be carried on without giving rise to diversity of result. Contexts, whether individual, social or cultural, differ too much for it to be otherwise. There has to be acceptance of such diversity as a strength rather than a weakness. No other approach to theological enquiry has any chance of being adequate to present needs, if intelligent witness is to be made to either religious realities or theological truthfulness. In the world of Everyman, including Christian Everyman, as in the world of the wider theological enterprise, there need be nothing tentative in such a statement if only as a response to facts: there can scarcely have been a time of such indiscipline, such unprincipled theological fecundity as we now see around us. No doubt this very feature of our world helps to make the churches follow their instinctive path of resisting any such conclusion. Yet the churches need to embrace diversity willingly, as a condition of present truthfulness and as the proper framework for freedom.

However, for all the force of these principles, there is no denying that freedom is, for any religion, both a welcome gift and a terrifying danger. There is always the twin need not to lose sight of the opening charismatic moment, when innovation occurred and freedom was enlarged, and, at the same time, to live with the tradition which in wisdom interprets that moment and usually seeks to 'freeze' both it and the interpretation of it. There is strictly no illogicality in that dual policy (impossible as it is to carry out in practice, for change and novelty seduce the most traditional of us; and the sanity of many is preserved because they do not even realize it!). No illogicality, but a great deal of tension and spiritual contradiction. It is hard to dwell upon the power of the charismatic moment (in the Christian case, the impact of Jesus), and at the same time not be moved oneself to creative vitality of mind and soul – and to feel that is God-given. We live in a period of extreme difficulty: on the one hand, the possibility of detailed, sensitive awareness of the Christian tradition, and of its constant flux, has never been greater: no one can now realistically see it as static, as a 'faith once delivered to the saints' and then simply transmitted down the years; on the other hand, the virtual death of the Christian culture means that extreme ignorance and confusion are all around. The one realization presses us towards development of Christian belief, now as hitherto, and perhaps gives us a certain confidence in judging where appropriate innovation may come, though, in the end, we must act and trust. To be aware of the tradition is to have gained the skill and modest assurance of which I spoke. The other realization, however, bewilders and shocks us into drawing lines of resistance and constraint. And the fact that the ignorance and confusion are strong within the churches themselves makes the drawing of the lines often crude and inept. The arguments adduced by so-called traditionalists against the ordination of women are sufficient evidence of that!

The New Testament affords an example of a dilemma not unlike our own in some ways. John 16.13 contains the statement that the Spirit 'will guide you into all truth'; and the question is: is that promise one of innovation or of preservation? Whose heart is it meant to warm, the liberal's or the conservative's? Is it a promise that the Spirit will disclose new insights and guarantee (but how?) their validity? Or a promise that the given truth will be maintained despite changes of form? I suspect it was intended by the Johannine writer and his community as the latter, in the face of the risks of the former and perhaps charges of novelty already engaged in, at which the writer felt a degree of guilt. For here was a Christian group which, manifestly to our eyes, had developed the tradition of Jesus' teaching and deeds in its own way and by the use of its own language and ideas. There is every likelihood that, whether from some of its own members or from other Christians, it was accused of using its freedom illegitimately to alter what had been handed on. At the same time, the writer saw his doctrine (including the very saying which is in question) as doing no more than bring out the truth in the tradition: it was legitimate exegesis of what had been received and what Jesus had stood for – and the Spirit would make it so.

We who engage in the theological enterprise have grown less trustful of that way of proceeding: for who can arbitrate between conflicting claims to be faithful to the tradition and to be following the Spirit? And who can be sure when exactly Christian identity is left behind, in past, present or future? But there is a modified and perhaps equally religiously mature sense in which we may learn from the Johannine situation: that is, we are to trust God as we make our conscientious judgements in the statement of theology, but without being too anxious about our correctness or validity; for correctness and validity are less applicable in this area than theologians have often believed and hoped. If we need to give ourselves advice in the present situation, we might say simply: more thought, less fear.

3
Daring to Study the Bible

What are biblical scholars for, as far as the Church is concerned? At one time, the position was straightforward, at any rate in theory. Their work was central to the business of theology, and theology's task was to elucidate and expound the faith of the Church. It was a task carried out essentially, and almost exclusively, within the Church, from a position of commitment. Especially in the Churches of the Reformation, the important role of biblical scholars in theology meant a considerable overlap, even a blurring, of biblical scholarship and theological thought. Scholars might expect to be listened to on matters of belief on the basis of their work on the Bible, simply because of an assumption concerning the Bible's authority in arriving at belief. To take a classical example, J. B. Lightfoot's work on *The Epistle to the Philippians* (first published in 1868) led him to write an influential statement[1] about the origins of the Church's ministry which contained unmistakably doctrinal ideas. On this view of their role, biblical scholars were part of a co-operative enterprise, conducted in the Church with the intention of deepening the Church's understanding of its faith. On some matters, such as Christology, their contribution amounted to the exposition of the early stages of the Christian faith to which later generations then added detail and precision. On others, such as the ministry, they might point out emphases and orientations in the light of which later developments might properly be even adjusted or corrected. In such a benign world, biblical scholars were no threat to established belief, and their conclusions were certainly not irrelevant, even if some of their working was of mainly technical interest. They were valued members of a team.

This almost paradisal situation no longer exists. In fact, it is a mistake to suppose that it ever existed perfectly once biblical scholarship became a serious discipline in the nineteenth century. Even in England, where it corresponded more to reality than elsewhere, what struck biblical scholars, working with biblical ideas, as a reasonable way of re-stating traditional belief, seemed to theologians who did not share their training to be rank and dangerous novelty. Charles Gore found this as he experienced H. P. Liddon's reaction to his ideas on Old Testament history and the incarnation;[2] nobody now thinks Gore a far-reaching radical.

The situation has changed largely because the universities, and biblical scholarship within them, have moved away from the Church. Most biblical scholars are Christians and devote some of their energies to 'helping the Church', but their professional responsibility is to the secular university or, if that is not their place of employment, to an academic ethos set by the university: that is, to an ideal of 'pure' scholarship, to rigorous standards and specialized interests. It is none of their professional business to have an eye on consequences for faith or possible contributions to general theological understanding. Not that they have an interest, either, in being destructive of faith or challenging to traditional beliefs. The whole matter is simply not their professional concern, whatever some of them may, rather boldly, do as individuals. It is not often that a work of biblical scholarship causes as much as a ripple in the religious or even the wider theological world. When such a thing now occurs it is usually because some eccentric or outrageous historical proposition has appeared: that Jesus did not exist, for example, or that he was as much a guerrilla leader as a prophet of God. In other words, it takes a maverick among biblical scholars to make much of an impact on general religious and theological thinking; and then the reaction is the often wholly appropriate one of shocked incredulity. And sometimes the sober and sensible majority is tarred with the brush. It is as if the discourse of biblical scholarship, with all its maturity and refinement, has become largely incapable of appropriation when it comes to forming a general framework or pattern of belief and theological reflection.

The isolation of biblical scholarship has probably (if irrationally) helped to foster the belief that it easily runs into scepticism and is destructive of traditional belief, not just in the hands of its more notorious practitioners, but by its very nature. The truth is that, like any academic discipline, it is conducted in a constantly questioning spirit, alert to new evidence and new or better ways of looking at old evidence; but in itself it has no interest in either supporting or countering any particular theological beliefs. Of course, individual scholars, like other members of society, have their private beliefs about controversial subjects like miracle, but from a strictly professional point of view they cannot go beyond the interpretation of the text and such other evidence as may be available. That makes biblical study sound very innocent and pure, and of course there are instances where theological assumptions are so strong, and perhaps so far past conscious reflection, that corruption occurs within the strict work of the discipline.

What precisely does biblical scholarship aim to

achieve? Its task is neither more nor less than to 'hear' what a biblical author wished to communicate. It strives with every nerve to let him 'be himself'; that is, it strives to avoid forcing him, whether through ignorance, prejudice or anachronism, into a mould of our making, or perhaps the making of the Christian tradition at some other period. In that sense, the biblical scholar's attitude to the Gospel of Mark or the Epistle to the Romans is one of open-minded humility. He has no prior feeling about what Mark or Paul ought to have said, no doctrinal case for which they are required as advocates. His responsibility is solely to them, as he strains his ears towards them, endeavouring to shut out all distracting sounds.

Of course, this worthy aspiration is incapable of achievement. In ordinary conversation, I may go to great trouble to exclude my own preoccupations and beliefs in the endeavour to understand my companion and may indeed achieve understanding at the level of the dictionary sense of the words used. Nevertheless, I cannot avoid being my limited self in the encounter, failing to grasp aspects of the intended meaning through ignorance of the speaker's character, circumstances and thought, and intruding my own conception of the range of human feeling and experience. In that way, my 'hearing' is impaired. I give my own significance to what is said. With the best will in the world, I can do no other. In the case of texts, perhaps especially writings from remote cultures and times like those of the Bible, these factors apply severely; and all the more so, as many of these texts have played such a pervasive role over such a long period and probably in the 'hearer's' own life.

However, while these reflections must always put a brake on confidence, there is no need to be despondent. There is no case for hearing simply what we want to hear, simply because perfect comprehension of another's speech is unattainable. There are ways, chiefly various kinds of interrogation, by which incomprehension can be whittled down. So, if biblical scholarship is seen as an attempt to 'hear' what the biblical authors wished to 'say', its history and its present activities may be described as an ever widening process of interrogation. Thereby the risk of failing to hear has surely been reduced and areas of incomprehension have been eliminated. Scholars may be seen as asserting their own presuppositions less as they extend the range of their questions.

This optimistic idea is partly illusory. The various questions one may ask of a text, as sometimes of a companion in conversation, do not always yield a single composite picture. Instead, each may simply lead to the formation of its own picture, distinct from the others; not reconcilable with them, just different. They are alternative ways of viewing the text. This does not make the multiplying of questions less worthwhile, but it may make it less enriching than it seems at first sight. The questions do not all unequivocally work towards the clarity of 'hearing' and may not all apply to the object simply because they are in principle capable of being asked. Indeed, some of the answers which scholars think they hear in the text returning to them may come from false or non-existent voices; in reality, the text has nothing to say along those lines. To read a Gospel as a sheer literary structure, a sequence of words, ideas and images, regardless of the historical setting[3] produces a very different effect, a different sense of the work, from an enquiry into its social and ecclesiastical background. The two enquiries may seem not so much complementary as incompatible. Similarly, to read a Gospel as if its writer were a mere compiler of separate traditions, already formed and polished in verbal sequences, gives a very different picture from a reading based on the assumption that he was a creative author, making his own work out of such materials as came to him. Again, the pictures are more incompatible than complementary.[4] Still, in principle interrogation is the only way forward and its general effect is to increase comprehension.

What does it mean to see biblical scholarship as the questioning of a text, the better to hear what its author intended to say? Each of the main aspects of biblical scholarship, almost all of them historical in their thrust, may be seen as one kind of question addressed to the text. What questions are they and what is their real value?

It is helpful to have a limited object in mind in order to achieve a clearer focus, rather than to envisage the vast and diverse material that makes up the Bible as a whole. In fact this procedure is not only helpful in increasing manageability; it is also itself suggested by an important result of biblical scholarship. If there is any sense in which that study has 'destroyed the Bible' (as is sometimes wildly alleged), it is in bringing about its breakdown into individual writings, each with its own time, place and setting of origin, within the life of whatever community produced it. There are still various attempts to hold on to, and even to revive, the concept of 'the Bible as a whole' and to resist seeing the collecting together of these books as, in terms of ordinary causation, historically fortuitous at many points. But this goes against the tide. Since historical criticism penetrated imaginatively through the mere statements of the text to the lives represented in it and at work in its formation, the whole direction of biblical study has been analytic, substituting for 'the Bible' the separate units of which it is composed. The fact remains that while a tradition of theological reflection and religious use hold them together, the emphasis has come to fall on them as distinct productions, each with its own voice or voices, and not as purposive contributions to a grand literary whole, somehow predetermined.

So let us have in view a Gospel, specifically the Gospel of Matthew. The Gospels after all have the advantages of being relatively familiar and of being the point where both clear and shadowy suspicions of biblical scholarship most commonly come to lodge. The record of the life of Jesus is doubtless the most sensitive historical area for Christians, who are concerned with belief in him and aware of belief's historical vulnerability. What questions may we ask of this Gospel?

Some are practical, like those on a form of application for a job or a passport. Addressed to the author, by way of the numerous manuscripts of all or parts of his work (the oldest dating from not much more than a century after the date of composition, which was about 85 AD): What did you actually write and where have later copyists mistaken or even deliberately altered your words? Addressed to the author, by way of the shape and structure of the book itself: What was your literary plan? How far was your work deliberately structured, how far haphazard? And by way of comparison with other related works, the Gospels of Mark and Luke: How does your material come to have so much in common with theirs, and what is the nature and order of dependence among you? The answers to these questions, none of which can be full and definitive, but all of which are extensive and illuminating, are required for a basic level of acquaintance and understanding.[5]

Other questions go much further: How much material concerning the life and teaching of Jesus did you have at your disposal, or (much more susceptible of an answer from the Gospel, our only source) on what basis did you select? How did you adapt material to fit into the work as a whole composition, and what was the framework of significance within which you placed it?[6] In these questions, the beginning and ending and the internal arrangement of episodes are being asked to reveal more than literary information. They will begin to disclose the writer's ideas and beliefs concerning his subject. So then we continue: What beliefs do you hold, about the world and the course of history, about God and Jesus, about the effects of Jesus' work? What is your theological 'picture'? More strictly historically: How do you stand on problematic issues for Christians of your day? For example, how do you see Jesus and the Church in relation to Judaism from which they sprang and which still surrounds you? And what is the way of life, what the needs and the problems, of the Christian community which you represent and for which you write?[7]

To all these questions the writer may, through his book and perhaps (though scarcely at all in our case) through external evidence, give answers of greater or lesser certainty, which enable us to 'hear' him. The biblical scholar's responsibility is discharged when he simply makes available what he has heard. In that sense, his attitude to those who ask him for the fruit of his labour is, politely, one of take it or leave it. Or perhaps: Here is what may be heard; go and, if you will, draw your own conclusions for your life (as an individual or as a church) as I draw mine. In other words, it is not his *professional* business or skill to suggest what effects it may have on them. *He* must return constantly to more questioning, more listening, for, by its nature, it is never a completed work.

But what might the effect be? Everything depends, now at one remove, again on the matter of 'hearing'. How willing is the recipient of the offerings made by biblical study to let Matthew (for example) be himself and say what he wished to say? Must he say only what the recipient has, by various routes, come to think that he said – that is, before any serious attempt to 'hear'? In theory, this is a curious, though not uncommon, expectation: it is settling in advance what careful enquiry may show. Prejudice is the word.[8]

34

Biblical scholars may now develop a little asser-
tiveness. Aware that often their enquiries are less
conclusive than they would wish, they may nonetheless
claim certain achievement. They may, for example, find
it a matter of positive progress to believe that each
Gospel has to be considered (that is, each author heard)
in its own right. Gone are the days when our knowledge
of Jesus could be seen as derived from an amalgam of the
contents of all four Gospels, with discrepancies felt as a
minor awkwardness. Whatever use they made of others,
the Gospel of Matthew and the rest are each distinct
works, saying what their authors wished to say; and
there is every reason to see the discrepancies as resulting
from intentional changes, expressing ideas and so dis-
closing the author at work. Gone too are the days when
the Gospels could be read as but innocent transmitters of
plain history, bringing Jesus' words directly (barring,
presumably, translation from Aramaic into Greek) to our
ears. Whatever their undoubted links with the time of
Jesus, they are all the result of partly overlapping and
partly independent lines of transmission and development, wherein his words and deeds were seen through
many different eyes and recounted by many different
tongues before they reached relatively stable form
within the setting given by an evangelist. At each stage,
both oral and written, intended meaning and received
sense took distinctive form, always, even in the narrow
span of years between Jesus' life and the writing of the
Gospels, inevitably producing theological movement.[9]

Gone are the days when we can read the Gospels as if
they were the work of people of our own time, with our
criteria of truth, our (in effect 'my') way of regarding the
world, alive to our distinctions and standards of evidence. The fact that we may be fellow participants with
them in the Christian tradition does nothing to render
their world less alien to us and only serves to domesti-
cate them, usually naively and thoughtlessly, to our

35

time.[10] There is no greater reason for expecting the Gospel of St Matthew to be capable of being understood as if written in our day than for us to be able to quit our 'world' and aspire, as if by time-machine, fully to comprehend reality through his eyes. In the cause of 'hearing' him, we are required to approach his world and, as far as possible, follow the flow of his mind; but such a move is always an excursion, self-consciously undertaken. We may often not be able to see just as we saw, but we can be in a position to say: He cannot have seen things *thus* or intended his readers to draw *such* a conclusion. In this way, we can be sure that the use in Matthew 28.19 of what we read as a trinitarian formula does not betoken the presence in the author's mind of 'the doctrine of the Trinity', that way of conceiving of the Christian understanding of God that developed in the subsequent period and in a framework quite other than the heavily Jewish mentality of this evangelist. It is to be understood in terms compatible with what we know from the Gospel as a whole and from comparable contemporary writings.[11] Of course the words were seminal for the later doctrine, in that they came to be read as authoritative Scripture and as Jesus' own words, but that later doctrine came to formulation in its own different intellectual setting. Of course there are also continuities of religious understanding between Matthew and the later thinkers (and, for that matter, ourselves), but continuities are not identities, and the attempt to see differences and developments is part and parcel of the duty to 'hear', essential if both Matthew and his successors are to be allowed to 'be themselves'.

Comparable questions arise in relation to the stories of Jesus' birth and resurrection, both of which appear in the Gospel of Matthew. Biblical scholars are bound to say that there is little evidence for either which is not derived from the writings found in the New Testament; that is, no appeal *a priori* to a doctrinal pattern in which they find a logically appropriate place can be allowed, for such patterns have no other possible ultimate basis than those same documents. They must also point to the element of impenetrability in the gospel accounts; that is, whatever we may surmise or even know about earlier tradition, it is in its totality strictly inaccessible.[12] What is before us is the text of Matthew and all we can hope safely is to elucidate *his* meaning. The *events* described, supposing there to be 'events', are shrouded in obscurity. Even taking the witness of all the sources, this obscurity is notably dense in the case of the resurrection: Who can say what precisely is supposed to have occurred? It goes without saying that a reader may *believe* the Gospel to give a straightforward and accurate record of wonderful happenings; yet biblical scholars have no qualification to tell us what happened several decades before the writing of the document before us, but only to enable us to 'hear' what the author intended us to hear by way of his words. But did he not mean us to take his stories as a record of past events? Is this scrupulosity not too fastidious by half?

At this biblical scholars can only urge care. Part of the business of 'hearing' Matthew is to enter into his outlook on history, his ways of handling stories, his sense of evidence and his convictions about God's activity in the world. The accuracy of this or that record can, strictly, be neither affirmed nor denied; but we can reach a context in which to make an informed judgement if we keep in mind two general points, one bearing more on the story of Jesus' birth, the other on the story of his resurrection. First, Matthew undoubtedly saw the story of Jesus from start to finish as a pre-ordained fulfilment of the old Scriptures, and in that sense read them backwards in the light of what had occurred. In practice, there was a dialogue of mutual influence in early Christianity between apposite scriptural texts and the telling of the story of Jesus. No one

can be wholly sure of the precise contribution of either
party in the dialogue to the stable written records of the
Gospels; nor can anyone reasonably doubt that the
dialogue took place from Christianity's earliest days. In
other words, Matthew was in a position to find or to
make stories about Jesus (who was the fulfiller of
Scripture because he was the agent of God), which he
owed, in whole or in part, to Scripture rather than to
events.[13] Scripture was his treasure house.[14]

Second, the belief in Jesus' resurrection was not in
New Testament times just a miraculous happening in
the sequence of Jesus' career, serving to vindicate him
at God's hand and to ensure his eternal triumph. It was
part and parcel of an apocalyptic world of thought and
imagery from which it cannot fairly be detached and
retain its original sense. 'Resurrection' was part of a
complex of conceptions which add up to the idea of a
new world to be inaugurated by God, a set of features
which would characterize that inauguration and its
sequel. Many of the early Christians were so filled with
the conviction that in and through Jesus the new world
was now present and available, and that no lesser terms
sufficed to describe the magnitude of what God had
done through him, that the language of resurrection
was naturally upon their lips – like talk of the Spirit and
of the Kingdom of God and of favourable judgement
given to God's faithful ones, all of which belonged
equally to the discourse about the new world. Biblical
scholarship cannot pronounce on the accuracy of stories
to the origin of which it has no privileged access. It can
only expound the stories as pieces of writing and
expressions of ideas, pointing to the intellectual and
religious context in which they belong. Thus, the
resurrection story appears as the account of an event
intelligible in its time and place, the outward objectifying of a recognized idea, and making sense in relation
to it.[15]

Therefore the biblical scholar has to speak a word of caution to those who isolate early Christian stories such as these from the literary and theological context in which their life dawned, and who, taking them in isolation, use them as building bricks in different structures of thought and belief; perhaps, for example, in seeing Matthew's birth story as 'essential' to a doctrine of the incarnation as *the* way to speak of the significance of Jesus, and the resurrection story as validating Christian existence or even life after death for everybody.

Biblical scholarship cannot be uninvented; and what can regretting it say of one's attitude to the world? As now practised, it cannot help stubbornly resisting (when consulted – left to itself it will not comment) all attempts to read the Bible anachronistically; to read back into its pages the beliefs and ideas, even about the Bible itself, that belong to later times; to read it as meaning what we now see that its writers, given their setting, could not have meant. The banishment and discrediting of anachronism are perhaps the most substantial and far-reaching achievements of biblical scholarship in the modern world. At first sight self-evident and innocuous, we should see that this has about it the character of dynamite.

The two examples that we have chosen illustrate general principles. It would have been possible to have selected other examples which would have seemed, from the point of view of traditional belief seen apart from modern biblical scholarship, harmless and in many cases simply fascinating. But the principles would have been identical. If they work in one case, they work in another; if they are inexorably valid *here*, their validity *there* must be accepted, whether it be welcome or not. There is virtue in examining a situation at its sharpest.

In the nature of the case, biblical scholarship is likely

to strike the relatively casual observer with traditional religious convictions as threateningly independent, or as constantly and primly voicing cautious and negative considerations. Its severely historical approach to Scripture and Christian origins accords ill with a credal view of Christian faith or one based on a sense of authoritative, providential and smoothly burgeoning development, and it seems to undercut them. Hard though it may be, it is necessary to choose in which direction truth lies. So it is no wonder that church life, and even preaching and the more intimate instruction of the faithful, have found it difficult to absorb either scholarship's methods or its conclusions: they have seemed too uncongenial, too discordant. Even when offering no threat or difficulty, the tone of scholarship has just felt wrong, irreverent. Analysis and cool attention to evidence are at variance with the disposition of devotion and growth in commitment, as with the ever insistent demand for religious certainty.

It is futile to apportion blame; it is better to understand why the supportive role of scholarship has been largely abandoned, and why church life has become so impervious to the methods and conclusions of biblical scholarship and to the implications for movement in the style and content of faith which may emerge from them. And this despite the vast effort devoted over many years to the education of the clergy and others in these very matters. Lurking somewhere here but still obscure, there is something approaching scandal and a deep crisis of integrity.

There is, however, a positive side. There are opportunities to be grasped by those with a mind to seize them. Let us follow up our previous examples: suppose that I 'hear' the Gospel of Matthew, and grasp his scriptural outlook, illustrated in his story of Jesus' birth, and his eschatalogical outlook, exemplified in the story of the resurrection; suppose that I 'see' *his* whole picture of Jesus, of which these are only parts, and, recognizing its coherence and power, willingly make an excursion into Matthew's world, identifying myself with the terms and pattern of his response to Jesus (for in his own way Matthew was trying to 'hear' Jesus, just as I try to hear Matthew, and Jesus by way of him); suppose that I recognize Matthew as only one among those whom I must hear, distinct voices not sharing his tones and differing in repertoire (Mark, for example, whose message and response were complete without a word on Jesus' birth and only the barest, most enigmatic statement of resurrection); may I not then draw certain conclusions not only about the Bible, but also about the nature of faith and the range of Christian possibilities open to me? At the very least, I may conclude that 'believing' may seem otherwise than as the acceptance of a body of revealed and unchanging truth. Rather, it may be a response of individual persons to God, in integrity, taking just account of all they can hold as true and of their whole setting in life, their 'world'. In this sense, faith and its expression in words and ideas, is a 'hearing' of God, analogous to the hearing with which biblical scholarship submits itself to the biblical authors. There is both an attempt at purity of response (it is to be God, and no self-made idol, that I seek to hear) and yet also a recognition of the self who does the hearing – a conditioned, limited self, for all his unfeigned hope for humility.[16]

There are other implications for Christian belief which may flow from the acceptance of biblical scholarship as a mode of reacting to the Christian Scriptures. An important one is the encouragement it seems to give to the development of Christian belief. Much of the work done by biblical scholarship in this century has had the effect, distinctly and cumulatively, of distancing the Bible from our own times and relativizing its forms of thought. So Jesus and the Gospels think thoughts and speak words appropriate to their time, and directly usable in our time only as impalpably domesticated through the operation of the Christian tradition. When an English choirboy sings the Psalms of David, with all the cultural trappings of an English service, he does not mean what the psalmist meant. Music, architecture and liturgical scenario as well as mental workings conspire to make that impossible and to create a world of meaning which must frankly claim its own validity, whatever mysterious sidelong connections it may have with the psalmist's sense. And the priest reading the gospel in a modern service, stuffed though he or she may be with exegetical knowledge, cannot do other than convey senses quite other than the evangelist intended. There is no impropriety here. There is, however, an appropriation, part aesthetic, part existential, which is simply different from the scholar's task of hearing and questioning. The scholar can claim no monopoly of the use of Scripture; but the distinctions need full recognition.

The firm placing of the biblical writings in their own times, and the impossibility of doing otherwise if their authors' meanings are our concern, leaves the modern reader no option, as he returns from his excursion to the Scriptures, but to do what each of the biblical writers did before they were bound up together in a single canonical volume: he must respond to God as he now can respond, do afresh the work which they did, and not feel too beholden to the whole continuous line of the Christian past with its twistings and turnings and its sheer unmanageable length. In this way biblical scholarship may have the salutary effect of setting not only the Bible, but also the flow of tradition, in a new and less dominating light; for tradition, too, in its successive phases, is in effect simply a series of merging attempts to make Christian judgements and to express Christian faith. The solemn avowal of mere faithfulness to the past, so constant in Christian history until recently, was anyway an illusion, made possible by ignorance, now much dispelled, of the realities of historical change.

These are considerations concerning fundamental attitudes to Christian belief itself. There are opportunities to be grasped also in relation to more specific matters. Enough has already been said about the essential context of particular aspects of Jesus' life as reflected in the Gospels in which they are described. A story does not tell of an isolable 'mystery', the backing for a dogma; it occupies a place within a total narrative presentation of Jesus, a statement in extended form concerning his whole import. For us too, then, it may be that faith consists not in the acceptance of particular items in the career of Jesus, however stupendous they may seem to be, however demanding of attention they may appear, but in response to his impact as a whole, in whatever way this response may be possible for us. In this perspective, Christian faith is response to God as seen in relation to Jesus and in relation to our own 'world' of perception.

Let us turn to another area. How much ecumenical argument is constructed on idealized notions of the early Church and comes to grief on rival claims about the structure of the early congregations? But suppose we see the life of these churches as related to the circumstances of their times, so utterly different from our own; and as related to those circumstances as a whole, so that the isolation of certain strands to serve modern theological purposes (as in the discernment of relationships between church offices then and now or the qualifications for their exercise) offends all historical (and common?) sense: why, then, should we not feel free to make judgements on these matters as the major thrusts of Christian understanding indicate, and not as early Christian history seems, so inauthentically, to prescribe? Here biblical scholars, if they could be given a chance, might give rise to a real liberation of the Church from the false shackles of its past, for vain and impious is the aspiration to perpetuate or restore what has been. Yet how pervasively (in liturgy or in church government) has that aspiration been embraced and its realization seen as the end of argument, and how anachronistic and fragmentary have been its fruits.

Ironically, it was biblical study in Reformation times which helped to forge those very shackles. For then the appeal to Christian origins, reflected in Scripture, itself offered the hope of liberation, willed by God, from the weight and dubiety of ecclesiastical tradition. But the service of the living God can never be conducted in terms of the past. The fearsomely relentless historical honesty of biblical scholarship at its best (could it dare to show itself more in the Christian marketplace) has the resources to provoke ordinary Christians into a much more realistic faith and service to God.

There is in all this one matter of still wider significance.[17] The innocent bystander, friendly to traditional faith, may reason thus: How can secular scholarship dare to give rise, even indirectly, to revisions in the content and processes of faith? Does not the Church, the ark of the truth of God, have its own sources for truth and its own modes of presenting it? The brief and shocking answer is *No. Mere* authority, in the Church as elsewhere, is a naked emperor. If one thing is now clear, there is no privileged *information* on matters relevant to faith which can enable pope or synod to know more than is wholly accessible to undergraduates investigating a given topic in the course of their humdrum, everyday degrees. The evidence is just *there*; and committees of worried Christians, with other than cool criteria of evidence on their minds, can do no better. Ah, but is there not the Spirit guiding the Church? Yes; but what is truth? And is not God's Spirit the Spirit of *truth*?

NOTES

1. *Dissertation on the Christian Ministry*, appended to the commentary and later published separately. It has been reissued as *Christian Ministry*, published by Morehouse-Barlow, Wilton CT.
2. For a convenient account of this episode, see G. Rowell, *The Vision Glorious* (Oxford 1983), ch. 10.
3. As in recent structuralist interpretation, contrasted here with the much older historical investigation, itself recently developed by the application of ideas and techniques drawn from sociology. For examples of each of these approaches, see G. Theissen, *The Miracle Stories of the Early Christian Tradition* (Edinburgh, T. & T. Clark, 1983), and H. C. Kee, *Christian Origins in Sociological Perspective* (London, SCM, 1980).
4. Here the contrast is between form criticism (classically exemplified in R. Bultmann, *The History of the Synoptic Tradition* [1921]; English tr., Oxford, Blackwell, 1963), and redaction criticism (see N. Perrin, *What is Redaction Criticism?* [Philadelphia, Fortress, and London, SPCK, 1970]. See also the essays in I. H. Marshall, ed., *New Testament Interpretation* (Exeter, Paternoster, 1977).
5. They have been the subject of abundant research, of which a résumé may most conveniently be found in the introductions to the commentaries, such as those by H. B. Green (Oxford 1975) and F. W. Beare (Oxford 1981).
6. For possible answers, again see the commentaries, and works such as J. D. Kingsbury, *Matthew: Structure, Christology, Kingdom* (London, SPCK, 1976); and his *Matthew as Story* (Philadelphia, Fortress, 1986); and M. D. Goulder, *Midrash and Lection in Matthew* (London, SPCK, 1974).
7. The great range of books on these matters may be approached through G. N. Stanton, ed., *The Interpretation of Matthew* (London, SPCK, 1983), and D. Senior, *What are They Saying About Matthew?* (Leominster, Paulist Press, 1983). See also P. S. Minear, *Matthew: The Teacher's Gospel* (London, DLT, 1984).
8. In 1860 there was published a liberal-minded book of theological papers called *Essays and Reviews* and its authors were in trouble for alleged heresy. One, Frederick Temple, future Archbishop of Canterbury, wrote to the then Archbishop, A. C. Tait, who had complained of him: 'Many years ago you urged us . . . to undertake the critical study of the Bible. You said that it was a dangerous study but indispensable . . . To tell a man to study, and yet bid him, under heavy penalties, come to the same conclusions with those who have not studied, is to mock him. If the conclusions are prescribed, the study is precluded.' (R. Davidson and W. Benham, *Life of A. C. Tait* (1891), I, 291; quoted in Noel Annan, *Leslie Stephen* (London, Weidenfeld & Nicolson, 1984), p. 207).
9. See W. H. Kelber, *The Oral and the Written Gospel* (Philadelphia,

Fortress, 1983); A. E. Harvey, *Jesus and the Constraints of History*, (London, Duckworth, 1982); and G. Vermes, *Jesus and the World of Judaism* (London, SCM, 1983); these deal from varied angles with aspects of the matters raised here.

10. On the issues raised briefly here, see D. E. Nineham, *The Use and Abuse of the Bible* (London, Macmillan, 1976).

11. On this example, see J. Schaberg, *The Father, the Son and the Holy Spirit* (Chicago, Scholars Press, 1982).

12. It is true, and important, that in relation to the resurrection (though not to the birth) we have earlier evidence than that of Matthew in the Gospel of Mark, which Matthew almost certainly used as a source, and the letters of Paul. But nothing takes us through stories to events, so as to answer anything like all the questions we should immediately like to ask about them.

13. See R. E. Brown, *The Birth of the Messiah* (London, Geoffrey Chapman, 1977); and the commentaries on Matt. 1—2.

14. Matt. 13.52.

15. See C. F. Evans, *Resurrection and the New Testament* (London, SCM, 1970); W. Marxsen, *The Resurrection of Jesus of Nazareth* (London, SCM, 1980).

16. See further J. L. Houlden, *Patterns of Faith* (London, SCM, 1977), and *Connections* (London, SCM, 1986).

17. See P. L. Berger, *The Heretical Imperative* (London, Collins, 1980) esp. on the now inevitable replacement, in matters of belief, of *authority* by *choice*.

4
Trying to be a New Testament Theologian

My question is: what can the study of New Testament theology contribute to the study and formulation of Christian doctrine, that is, to the theological task in the wider sense? There is no denying that the subject is at present problematic. It was formerly the crown of the New Testament scholar's career to write a theology of the New Testament, comprehending in a unified vision the ideas hitherto put forward in relation to discrete topics but now seen as contributions to a whole. Even when death or exhaustion has not supervened, there has been a decline in the number of those trusting their wisdom enough to undertake such a project, and some would not now see it as part of their craft.

It is not simply a question of trusting one's wisdom. The subject itself has long been more than a little ambiguous. Is New Testament theology[1] simply one aspect of the rigorously historical study of these writings, limiting itself to a descriptive role? Or is it a kind of theology, setting out to give an account of Christian doctrine as revealed and normative, but in terms related to and based upon the New Testament? Even when it sets out on the former path, it has a way in practice of straying on to the latter;[2] but at the level of theory the ambiguity remains. The most severely historical kind of New Testament theology in fact has a doctrinal role, if only in stimulating the imagination theologically. So it may be that New Testament theology is always something of a hybrid, even if only by implication.

From the time when New Testament studies set up as an independent enterprise, and were released from merely backing up doctrine, New Testament theology has been not only of the descriptive but also of the theologically more positive kind, an account of the Christian faith from a New Testament perspective. So whatever the proportions of New Testament studies and doctrine may be, and whatever the precise nature of each in a particular case, New Testament theology is New Testament scholarship looking in some way in a doctrinal direction. It compels the specialists to turn their eyes towards a neighbouring field. If they do so now, they may be forgiven for shrinking back into the relative order and safety of their own familiar territory. The land of doctrine is not a tidy or a pleasant sight. Who knows on what principles matters are conducted there? Are its inhabitants committed to expounding the authoritative doctrines of Christianity, a body of belief achieved at Nicaea and Chalcedon or Trent or Vatican II? Are they interested in the New Testament evidence in a manner dictated by the items of the dogmatic theologian's traditional agenda?[3] If so, then the New Testament scholars feel a professional unease: they feel that the achievements of the dogmatic process in Christian history were in various ways parasitic on the New Testament, and they are conscious that their present ways of handling it threaten the methods whereby those doctrinal beliefs were reached. There is a risk of gaff-blowing, even of calling in question the whole business of forming theology on the basis of the New Testament.[4] It is not a thing for a courteous visitor to do.

Or are those who live in the land of doctrine

committed to something much closer to philosophy of religion? In that case, New Testament scholars find it hard to discover a point of attachment, yet they know that such a point must be found. Neither their professional equipment nor the documents which are the subject of their study give them much skill when it comes to such fundamental doctrinal reasoning. It is outside their reach; for however great their academic detachment, in so far as they are practitioners of the Christian tradition, they work from the inside.

In fact, all the doctrine-dwellers (so it seems to outsiders) act according to their own lights. Compared to New Testament scholars, they seem an anarchic lot. Even within a single church tradition, the subject appears to lack clear criteria, even clear subject-matter. Where it is (essentially even if disguised) commentary on decisions and formulations arrived at elsewhere, then it is plainly a dependent enterprise; and, unless there is to be an assumption of divine guidance transcending human activity, its purity is marred by knowledge of the political and cultural factors affecting the process by which the formulations came to birth. Dogmas do not drop from heaven any more than Scriptures. Where it is more abstract or independent in its stance,[5] then it is liable to be more or less cut off from that church setting which, whatever its inconveniences, seems to be doctrine's proper location.

Sometimes, doctrine seeks to be a looser, more varied pursuit than I have so far recognized. It may reckon to draw on resources of many kinds, in effect from the general intellectual climate. There will be a broad dependence on the prevailing philosophical atmosphere, a recognition of 'what cannot now be said by reasonable people'. There will be an awareness of the appropriate church tradition, and probably of the Christian tradition as a whole. There will be sensitivity to hermeneutical procedures, enabling the past and the present to be stirred into the mixing-bowl from which acceptable doctrine may emerge.[6]

Doctrine scholars of this persuasion are hopeful and co-operative by disposition, and of all styles of doctrinal study this one is the most likely to turn, in a spirit which both gives and seeks sympathy, to New Testament scholarship. Starting from the other side, such doctrine scholars as these are the nearest counterpart to the New Testament theologians, those most likely to listen to their voice and not seek simply to bend them to their predetermined needs. It is true that they have other bridges, too, to build and maintain, but they cannot avoid the search for some satisfactory way of regarding and then using the New Testament, both as a collection of writings from the start of the Christian tradition and as a powerful presence throughout that tradition's course. There is no avoiding the conclusion, however, that if doctrinal scholars seek such help, they are likely, in present circumstances, to go away either empty-handed or with a gift of raw, undeveloped material unaccompanied by instructions for its use. If the land of doctrine looks to would-be New Testament theologians bewildering in its uncertainty and diversity, New Testament scholars easily seem naive and unreflective when they aspire to theological activity. They keep running for cover in enclosed historical or linguistic investigations. They will not come out with clear guidance on what is to be done with their deliverances. And when they speak theologically, not only are they too wedded to New Testament words and ideas, but they seem unwilling to reckon with so many considerations which are plainly important theologically.[7] Sometimes they just disclaim responsibility, in a way which the doctrine scholars find feeble and infuriating, for it impedes their own work.

There are of course reasons more domestic to New Testament scholarship itself for the reticence which attends the pursuit of New Testament theology. Everything pushes in the direction of work and perception which are analytic and historically limited – analytic and particularized as more attention is legitimately given to the theological outlook of individual New Testament writers and less to ideas and terms across the New Testament as a whole. If the New Testament is treated thus, what can a New Testament theologian contribute but an account of each of the writers in turn? Historically limited, as the life and thought of the New Testament period are perceived with increasing vividness and fulness and with the aid of ever sharper tools such as those derived from sociology and anthropology, all these trends reduce interest in and facility for handling the New Testament as the fount of a tradition and as itself a witness to theological truth.

However, in some aspects of redaction criticism and other associated techniques of gospel study, there is intensified pressure in a clearly theological direction. What is not so evident, at least at first sight, is how this brand of theological interest, rigorously historical as it is, can contribute to New Testament theology in any comprehensive sense, especially if such theology is itself to contribute to theology understood more widely. Still, there is undoubtedly here a lever upon which we may seek to lean in order to shift the dead weight that now inhibits New Testament theology from movement. In due course, I shall make use of it.

The overwhelmingly historical orientation of New Testament studies is not only a deterrent to the pursuit of New Testament theology in principle. It is also the source of dissatisfaction with such attempts as have been made in the past. Those who have done New Testament theology by the apparently direct method of distinguishing and relating themes found in the writings themselves, usually attributing a key role to some among them, have fallen victim to increased sensitivity to the culture-bound nature of those themes, as they are expressed in first-century words and ideas.[8] To work with those ideas and words in propounding theological patterns for today is to impose upon them senses and connections which they never had in the New Testament itself and to make assumptions about the canon which need bold argument if they are to avoid the charges of anachronism and arbitrariness.

The brave attempt to distil from the New Testament a theology for our times which goes by the name of demythologization runs into comparable difficulties. For the New Testament writers, what *we* may call the essence of their teaching and the myth in which, to our eyes, it was clothed formed a unity. There must then be now a sense of impropriety in severing the one from the other and claiming the palatable aspects of the New Testament writers' work (and usually in fact that of only a selection of them) as a fair account of New Testament theology. In that way, while it avoids the mere retailing of New Testament words and ideas, a programme of demythologization falls equally under the charges of anachronism and arbitrariness.[9] From another angle, it is yet one more in the long line[10] of accounts of New Testament teaching which ruthlessly impose upon it a later viewpoint, perhaps highly commendable in itself but found appealing on other grounds besides its supposed presence in the New Testament.

If recent experience is anything to go by, there seems to be no way of escaping from the extreme difficulty of making legitimate use of the New Testament theologically if we are at the same time to be faithful to historical method. Where attempts have been made to present the theology of the New Testament, it now often seems that there was a blurred historical focus, some degree of failure to reckon with the writings in their own right and in their own setting. This is not simply an intellectual failure, something to earn a historian's rebuke. It is also a moral failure; for it involves a refusal to hear what the ancient writer wished to say, an insistence that he speak to our condition and dance to our tune. Even if we stick close to his words, they are almost inevitably bent to needs and purposes other than those of their original setting, often by the mere fact of their removal from the total social and cultural context in which they were written.

It is possible to cut the knot by the simple expedient of dropping faithfulness to historical method when it comes to making theological use of the New Testament documents, and so confining historical work on them to its own strict and narrow concerns. It may be done not, as so often, by sheer inadvertence or out of some atavistic dogmatism, but in a spirit of high sophistication.[11] We may hold that the New Testament is a text, words on paper, which we should receive and attend to simply as they strike us. Interpretation is then not an academic but an aesthetic experience, though no doubt with subsequent moral or intellectual effect. If I read the story of the walk to Emmaus, I am not to immerse myself in questions about its possible source and literary affinities, its vocabulary and place in Lucan thought or among the resurrection stories. Such concerns will divert me from it simply as a text, push me into matters which lie behind it rather than within it. Rather, I must let the text as text work its will with me, seize me if it can, and move me by the sheer power of its structure and wording: thus will its message be heard. We note that there is here no strictly theological interest. It is not a matter of reversion to the uncritical use of texts in support of doctrines. If there is theological fruit from this approach, then it is inchoate, indirect, and by way of the stimulation of the theological imagination.

New Testament scholars will not easily content themselves with such a solution – for both the worst and the best of reasons. The worst of reasons is fear of the elimination of New Testament scholarship from the business of theological interpretation. If New Testament scholarship were to be mainly confined to purely historical exegesis in its various aspects – and this is perilously near to being the case – then there would be a serious price to pay at the practical level: in terms of even greater isolation from other theological disciplines, the loss of any claim to what may, in a Benthamite spirit, be called usefulness, and ultimately an intelligible threat from the paymasters of the academic world: for why should this little collection of first-century texts, if that is the perspective in which they are deliberately and exclusively being viewed, merit more than a pittance from any public or private coffers, more than a fraction of the academic resources still devoted to them?

Fear is a low reason for discontent with the removal from theological reflection on the New Testament of historical study in its many aspects. A higher reason is a conviction that the understanding of the historical realities involved in the composing of a text is an enrichment to general appreciation and neither an impediment nor a diversion. Not only is it a brake upon sheer error but there is, not necessarily but potentially, a continuum between historical knowledge and even the quasi-aesthetic and very personal 'grasping' of the text which I described. Such knowledge constitutes a salutary discipline which purifies and enhances rather than impedes appreciation.

If then we exclude the dropping of historical method as a satisfactory way out of our difficulties, it remains inadequate to withdraw, in deference to that method, from serious theological concern. There is indeed one peculiarly problematic reason for discomfort in settling for the self-sufficiency and self-containedness of the historical study of the New Testament. It is the question of the relation of the New Testament to the Christian tradition subsequent to it and, in various ways and degrees, dependent upon it. Putting it more sharply, it is also the question of the relation of such studies to the Church. Historically, that relation has in this respect served New Testament scholarship well, despite all that may be put on the debit side. It is plainly a fact that if it had not been for the belief that the study of the New Testament was necessary to the Church, especially in the training of its clergy, the subject would not have the prominence which it still enjoys in many theological faculties and departments; and it is arguable that, if it should depend on justification on that ground, it no longer merits its present prominence. Largely through forswearing anachronism academically in the interests of historical realism, its own position has itself become an anachronism! But that is, once more, mere politics, a matter of pragmatic observation, and we need not necessarily feel a sense of obligation because of the history of our subject. There is the more substantial question of the relationship of New Testament studies to the Christian tradition. Leaving to the historians its purely historical aspects, how are we to understand and handle that relationship? Is there any relationship which falls to our responsibility, and if so, how are we to discharge it? Here, if anywhere, New Testament theology may surely find a place as a distinct, reputable and perhaps obligatory subject.

One possibility is that we should adopt a sweet-and-sour approach and give the historians their head – in a theological spirit. It is not a common view, but we may hold that each Christian period (including the first period of all), of course overlapping with those before and after it, has validity in its own right, and, theologically and morally, neither owes debts to its predecessors nor has authority over its successors. It simply 'happened', as a stage along the providential way. Yet it is hard to be content with that procedure as far as the New Testament period is concerned. To put the matter at its least demanding level, while the Christian religion remains in some sense a faith derived from and dependent upon Jesus and does not see itself as simply freewheeling through history, the New Testament witness to him has a privileged position – even from a purely empirical point of view and apart from theological considerations. It is possible for Chalcedon, Trent or Calvin's *Institutes* to be seen as points along the way rather than authorities, in a way that the New Testament writings cannot be. However historical and relativistic the regard we bring to them, they have had and have not wholly lost a defining role in the Christian tradition – difficult though it may be to describe satisfactorily. It follows that New Testament studies will fail in so far as they do not take account of that role. No doubt they can, in their most self-contained mood, find justification in terms of the pursuit of truth and so fend off marauding vice-chancellors; but that will not remove the claim exercised by their actual place in Christian tradition and by present-day Christian theology as it looks to them, insistently yet obscurely, for help. The difficulty is to see how that claim can be met without doing violence to the integrity of historical study as it is now perceived.

It is time to attempt a positive view of the pursuit of New Testament theology in present circumstances. Certain principles may be laid down. First, no account will be satisfactory which imposes on the New Testament the later doctrinal agenda of the Church. It is historically artificial and anachronistic to undertake a study of, for example, the New Testament witness to the classical doctrine of the Trinity or of the Immaculate Conception. The shrinking of Protestant scholars (at least) from the one does not always prevent them from being attracted to the other. Neither is admissible. It is of course possible to identify elements of New Testament thought or texts within the New Testament which, as a matter of fact, played a part in the development and eventual formulation and defence of either doctrine, or else, with hindsight, may be seen to adumbrate that development, but that is a different matter from 'witness'. Only a Newman-like view of the New Testament writers, seeing them as in some way, even unconsciously and indefinitely, imbued with the whole doctrinal edifice of Christianity, would justify such an approach.[12]

Second, no account will be satisfactory which treats the New Testament as having a corporate mind. Such a procedure, drawing upon all its components at will, may be possible for those of high canonical principle, but no longer can it hope to win wide acceptance; and the very fact that it must be argued for with difficulty and cannot assume a position of natural command makes a radical difference to its status. While it is legitimate to trace possible influences (though they are rarely crystal clear) from one New Testament writer to another, even to the point of suggesting trajectories of ideas which develop as they speed through early Christian space, the weight must fall on the particular minds at work in the writings and their identification.[13] Unless we are deliberately to risk a clouded view, there is no going back from the theology of Mark, Matthew or Luke to 'the theology of the Synoptic Gospels' – however strong our belief in Q as a force within two of them. It may turn out that a particular writing will not yield to interpretation as the work of a single author, but must be the product of a number of not wholly compatible minds. Nevertheless, the writing as it stands, however it reached its present state, represents a certain fusion of minds which once interacted, albeit imperfectly, in a way that the canonical collection as a whole does not.[14]

A weaker form of the 'corporate New Testament mind' approach may still appear to be valid. Surely a term like 'Kingdom of God' or 'Lord' or 'saviour', found in a number of different New Testament writings, has a meaning, or cluster of meanings, which makes it possible to discuss it independently of a particular writer and in a consideration of New Testament theology as a whole. Such a discussion forms a legitimate step after the elucidation of such terms in relation to the contemporary Jewish or Hellenistic background. But, as far as the New Testament is concerned, it is only a step on the way to the only plain reality before us – a series of discrete texts and contexts. However thorough our general understanding of 'Kingdom of God', interpretation has to reckon with *this* writer's meaning in *this* specific setting within *his* work as a whole. The unit is not the term itself but the theological thought of the writer who uses it.[15]

Third, no approach will be satisfactory which wilfully neglects the total cultural context of either the New Testament writers or the modern interpreter. Perhaps what is required in this respect is not so much the achievement of perfection as the provision of a brake on foolishness. New Testament theology has suffered much from the attribution to theological ideas in the New Testament of a kind of timelessness and the bestowing on texts, originally transient in their significance, of eternal seriousness.[16] New Testament theology, more than any other branch of New Testament study, finds it hard to abandon the belief that, in some fairly strong sense, Scripture was written for *our* learning. Awareness of cultural context is much the most effective antidote to such belief, though it works less by countering than by bypassing it. The outcome is a sense of distance[17] between the original context and our own, which at first sight inhibits anything other than a descriptive theological account and on any showing compels doctrinal reflection which is filtered and indirect.

These principles appear to present a massive deterrent to any theological work with the New Testament that is other than analytic and descriptive. They seem to forbid any movement out from New Testament study in a doctrinal direction of a general or synthesizing character. At most, they might license a theologically vague inspirational force from the New Testament to us, a carrying-over of sentiment, exercising over us no kind of control. Yet anything lacking these features falls under the condemnation of ignoring historical realism – and the disadvantages of that are only too obvious.

Edward Schillebeeckx, in his two books *Jesus* and *Christ*,[18] adopts what is essentially a pragmatic as much as a theoretical approach. To be recognizable as well as legitimate, Christian theology must work with two interests in mind, move between two poles: on the one side, Christian origins, the pristine expressions of faith, and on the other side, the present setting within which, in all its complex appreciation of truth, faith must now operate. It is uncertain whether this is better described as the work of a New Testament theologian determined to be fully open to the present context of doctrinal statement or of a dogmatic theologian determined not to force the New Testament evidence into an historically alien mould. In effect, he stands squarely with one foot on either side of the divide; and though, from the standpoint of New Testament studies, his work lacks a certain sharpness of historical focus, at least the principle of the limited historical context of the New Testament writings is fully accepted. Such an approach is pragmatic in the sense that a Christianity which ignores its origins seems bound to lack definition and identity.

But how, in Schillebeeckx's account, are the two poles

connected? Not, it appears, by attributing authoritative status to the continuous process of Christian theological development which links them at the temporal level. That would be to court incoherence and intellectual suffocation. It is Christian origins and the ever-changing Christian present which specially merit Christian theological attention; and the link is, once more partly pragmatically, to be found by way of key features which dominate the early Christian scene: the conviction of Christ as living, the awareness of 'salvation', and the sense of a new, expectant community of God's people. Those beliefs form the essential legacy of earliest Christianity, as witnessed in the New Testament, and the essential reality of any Christianity worthy of the name now or, presumably, at any time.[19]

Such a view has much to be said for it. It avoids the narrowness of some older biblical theology, with its closeness of working with biblical language and thought-forms; yet it preserves an intelligibly biblical vision. The pragmatic quality of this approach is attractive in that it helps bridge the gap between historical objectivity and particularity on the one hand and doctrinal truth on the other, which has proved such a chasm in the light of recent trends in New Testament studies. It provides a link between origins and the present while leaving the latter an undefined – perhaps because indefinable – measure of autonomy. The question of present doctrine is not to be answered solely by reference to the Christian past, even to Christian beginnings: work remains for us to do. Nevertheless, how it is to be answered remains obscure.

But the picture Schillebeeckx paints is not without hints for further progress; for it indicates certain lines of method. And the principles we laid down reinforce them. It is plain that earliest Christian theology did not spring ready-made from within the Christian movement itself. In all its forms, it represented an amalgam of elements, some drawn from the common stock of contemporary beliefs, some quite novel, resulting from the impulse of Jesus, others the unstable products of the impact of the latter upon the former, the effects of imperfect and only partly coherent reflection. But it was an amalgam which belonged to those unique circumstances.

Let me then propose, as a first contribution to doctrine from New Testament studies, viewed in the light of my principles, a sense of the relative autonomy of doctrine as a present pursuit. This is a devastating contribution indeed. Is not doctrine, by its very nature, bound to the tradition, and incapable of identity if severed from it? Its practitioners will vary in the degree of admitted or desired debt to the prevailing culture, but 'autonomy' is scarcely a word they readily allow to spring to their lips. Yet New Testament scholars, acting in their own right, now have a duty to bring it to their attention. New Testament scholars spend their lives studying the New Testament documents within their original context and quite regardless of their future destiny. They have no responsibility to see them as propelled towards Chalcedon or supporting Lutheran orthodoxy or tending towards the eucharistic teaching favoured by Vatican II Catholicism. If anything, they are likely to point to their alien quality in relation to later developments. They must, of course, acknowledge the force of tradition and the reality of continuity in belief and practice, but they canot forbear, as they look out towards the history of the Church, to indicate the measure of illusion which invariably afflicts those who claim to be in a tradition of faith.[20] Continuity of institution there may be, change and development of belief there always are. Whether because of sheer ignorance of times past or because of the irresistible pressure of new cultural assumptions, there is always change in the proportion, the perspective and the very content of belief. New Testament scholars are used to seeing the shift from Paul to the writer of the Pastoral Epistles or even Ephesians as already seismic. There is then every propriety in pointing to the great measure of autonomy each new theological generation exercises, even if it denies it with every breath and swears allegiance to the faith once delivered.

There is then the question: now that it has come to the surface, how may doctrine use this autonomy? It is one thing to exercise it unconsciously, the conscious mind being filled with thoughts of faithfulness to the past, quite another to feel the responsibility of exercising autonomy, within an undoubted continuity of life and witness. Is it a matter of defining in advance limits of adaptation, drawing up formulas for the legitimate translation of old beliefs into new forms, or finding criteria for distinguishing between essential and expendable, permanent and transient doctrines? New Testament theology has not lacked exponents of all these arts;[21] and often they have used them with a regrettable lack of candour or explicitness. Yet all suffer from superficiality and a lack of that historical realism whose demands can no longer be refused.

The recognition of such autonomy, as an inevitable condition of life, may fill the theologian with alarm. But his nerve may be restored by a second contribution from New Testament scholarship as it turns in the direction of the doctrinal task. Once more, it does not, initially, go beyond the bounds of factual observation. It consists of an analysis of the procedure by which earliest Christian faith arose. It is, be it noted, for this purpose a matter of procedure rather than of content. The New Testament scholar can offer a sight of that procedure at a stage in Christian history marked by relative simplicity, before the complexities arising from faithfulness to a developing tradition existed. Without in the least subscribing to myths of a golden age, we can say that it shows, from a conceptual point of view, a kind of pristine purity.

It is an over-simplification, yet far from being a falsehood or a gross distortion, to say that the Christian faith began with the impact of the career of Jesus (whether perceived as a whole or in terms of some part of it). It is an over-simplification because only the gnostic or Marcionite Jesus appears like a bolt from the non-historical blue. Of course we are concerned with his cultural and social antecedents and keen to understand him in the light of them. But no amount of such understanding succeeds in making him merge wholly into his background.[22] Nor is it simply the weight of later and possibly misguided faith which prevents his disappearance from the foreground. It is a matter of his immediate historical impact. It may be that his role was speedily inflated beyond all reason – that is a matter for argument – but the fact of substantial immediate impact, unrivalled among Jewish contemporaries who can be put forward for comparison, is undeniable.

Yet what is available to us as wholly incontrovertible and objective is (we must, however reluctantly, admit) only the *fact* of his impact. The very moment it is observable to us, from the response of those who felt and received it, subjectivity and diversity arose. We cannot penetrate behind the social, cultural and personal particularity of those receivers of Jesus. Of course, they are not in reality so diverse in their particularity that no intelligible picture can emerge and no statement, of greater or lesser probability, concerning the Jesus whose impact they experienced, can be made. But in principle, particularity, the contribution of the one who receives, enters in and can never again be banished.

It enters initially in the form of experience. This experience too is, strictly, hidden from us; in the purely factual sense that, with the possible and in any case

highly problematic exception of Paul, we have no access
to those who received the power of Jesus directly; also
in the sense that experience, in this sense, is inarti-
culate, inward, even powerful by virtue of its word-
transcending quality. Nevertheless, it can, however
hesitantly, be surmised and characterized.[23] It is not of
first importance for our purpose that we describe it
accurately, only that we identify the *fact* of it: there *was*
such subjectively conditioned experience. We may call
it, to use the most general terms, an experience of
salvation, of new well-being in relation to God. Its
precise nature would naturally depend on the pre-
existing need and disposition of those concerned. What
is more, it would be wholly limited by that need and
disposition. It may be in a particular case that only the
arousing of the experience of salvation really brought to
awareness a sense of need: did Paul see the Law as
inadequate except in the light of Christ?[24] Even so the
principle holds: a man experiences salvation, however
self-transcending it may enable him to be, only in terms
of his own existing equipment of mind and personality.
It was not open to Paul to feel the impact of Christ in
terms of *nirvana* or an assurance of a future preferential
migration of his soul, but only in some relation to the
Law which dominated the horizon of his dealings with
God.

Such experience is visible to us only through its
having received verbal, indeed written, expression.
That move brings further obliqueness.[25] While it makes
communication and permanence possible, it also brings
new limitation. It is true that, under the force of
profound experience, old words may be pressed into
new work;[26] but still, if a writer is to be intelligible, he
must use the stock of words available to him. More
precisely than at the stage of experience, he is the
creature of his setting: the creature and, from the point
of view of later times and of contemporaries who are

significantly different from him, tragically even the victim. Written expression is both a blessing and a curse. It leads to the sharing of experience, but also to its being objectified. Indeed, if the written words then go on to acquire formal authority, with the agreement of others who have not known the initial experience, they acquire, in relation to that experience, a distorting and a distancing role. They may command assent and inspire new experience, but they are heard with new ears and repeated by new lips. Church formulations are bound to have this character: negotiation and consensus mean a loss of immediacy to particular experience.

Blessing or curse, the process thus outlined is that by which Christian theology set off on its journey. It is a process constantly repeated ever since, whatever modifications and whatever increase in complexity are brought by the passage of time; especially as new expressions of faith create new experience and encapsulate the whole process in themselves. Each new repetition brings its own shifts, its own new injection of the particular, however unwilling and unaware. Theology, as an expression of faith, is ever creative and ever unfaithful to the tradition, if faithfulness is measured by fixity. May not New Testament scholarship urge upon doctrine the franker recognition, and then the welcoming, of this inevitable character of the doctrinal process and task, with its necessary autonomy and its innovatory role? It involves naturally a quite transformed attitude to the formulas and beliefs of the past. It will not be a matter of either guiltily striving to keep dying beliefs alive by some kind of reinterpretation or discarding them as if they had always been somehow erroneous. The expression of the experience of salvation is always more or less inadequate, and yet has within its context a certain validity; but it always tends to be more confident and less provisional in its claims than its content justifies. Even in the best hands, it is only an attempt to achieve the impossible. 'Autonomy' is then a serious word. There are no exemptions from its rule, no enclaves of doctrine exempt from its effects, no items of belief which come down to a later period immune from change and somehow sacrosanct, no predetermined key beliefs which have a right to persist at all costs.

Making the most of any standing we have so far obtained, we who begin from the New Testament side have a more threatening contribution to offer to those whose business is the elucidation and statement of doctrine (and indeed to ourselves when we extend towards that task). Our chief professional glory is our sensitivity to history, our feeling for the New Testament circumstances in themselves, with their variety and their strangeness. We cannot but offer that sensitivity both to those whose concern with other and wider periods or aspects of Christian life has not so far led them, as a group and a discipline, to share its keenness and to those whose interest is primarily not historical but the present statement of Christian doctrine. For the former, it is only a matter of time. It is unlikely that there will be any more reputable histories of Christian doctrine which neglect the social and cultural circumstances in which doctrine has come to birth.[27] Accounts of Christian belief which give an impression of disembodied timelessness or of the pure interiority of beliefs will cease to be acceptable. It is a process which can surely now be left to take its course. But it is less predictable that, without encouragement, those whose concern is the present statement of Christian doctrine will acquire reflective sensitivity to their own social and cultural formation and to its effect upon the doctrine they think and write.[28]

Suppose they are freed somewhat by recognition of the necessary relative autonomy of each period (indeed, each thinker and writer) in the interaction of experience and its formal expression; then it is a still harder step to state doctrine for oneself with a full sense of its transience and its deeply conditioned quality. Indeed, the recognition of such limitation may occasion the collapse of the enterprise or at the very least the muting of its confidence as doctrinal statement; and what is the good of Christian doctrine unless it is kerygmatic in tone and style? Not to go beyond elucidation is to run the risk of death. So the contribution of New Testament scholarship may turn out to be the demise of doctrine as a pursuit, at any rate as traditionally understood. All, it may seem at first sight, because of insistence on certain fundamental and pervasive points about method. New Testament scholarship presents the methods it has come to adopt, and simply claims that they are equally and necessarily applicable to matters of doctrine. Only an academic time-lag has prevented their use with comparable rigour in other spheres of theological study.

But to leave the matter at the level of method is to underestimate the seriousness of the contribution New Testament studies have to make to doctrine. It is also a matter of content. The historical sensitivity which New Testament scholars have so long cultivated leads to the realization that Christian belief changes from one period to another, not simply in emphasis, not by steady unfolding or more careful definition, but in shape and content, as one cultural environment gives place to another. Patterns of belief that centred on the coming end of all things were not simply adjusted, they died away. That crucial factor simply lost its dynamic and pervasive role. The centuries-long preoccupation of practical Christian belief with death, not only as the focus of piety but also as the matter in relation to which salvation and morals were inescapably considered, has become for very many Christians, including those who write doctrine, a thing of the past, no longer capable of playing its determinative part.[29] These shifts are as

significant as any that can be imagined. They have
not been the result of conscious reflection in the
Christian community at either the popular or the official
level; on neither question has any change of teaching
been promulgated. Yet it is hard to think of any matters
in relation to which such shift of belief is more pro
found in its effects on the whole Christian doctrinal
identity.

The effect is to give to doctrine in any period a more
constructive role and a greater responsibility, and at the
same time a more experimental tone. It can have no
expectation of finality, just as it cannot reckon merely to
restate the inherited beliefs of the past. It cannot see
itself as momentous, and can feel a certain freedom in
reacting to the circumstances of the time. At the same
time, its scope may be dramatically reduced and
simplified.

Sheerly at the factual level, Christian theology, to be
recognizable, must attend to its beginnings in relation
to Jesus. We outlined the pattern of those beginnings
from a theological point of view. It was a matter of
response to Jesus and of the expression of experience to
which he gave rise. Making allowance for the
strangeness, to us, of the thought-forms and terminology used, we may feel a certain simplicity in that
process. It was a far cry from the structure of distinct but interlocking beliefs that later came to constitute Christian doctrine. There was, in essence, just a
range of ways of responding to Jesus as the decisive
agent of God, or, to put it more formally but already
perhaps too woodenly, a range of christologies within
the setting of a range of eschatological patterns and
images. In the terms of later formal doctrine, and so
anachronistically, Christology, soteriology and eschatology filled the picture. The rest of so-called doctrine
was really the application or extension to other matters
of this central conviction about Jesus. Even to refer to

the New Testament faith as 'doctrine' is to risk importing formal and structural considerations that are wholly alien to the situation.

In that sense, the message of New Testament studies to doctrine is a counsel of simplicity and the warning that much of alleged doctrinal debate may be factitious and misconceived. In the light of the concerns of the New Testament and its conception of what constitutes Christian belief, what intelligible basis can there be for the controversies about the sacraments or the ministry or the nature of the Church which have long been so high on the doctrinal agenda? The sense in which these matters are 'theological' can only be in relation to the question: What are the implications of the mission of Jesus, and the understanding of God derived from him, for these matters in the context of the present life of his followers? There is no 'timeless revelation' on these matters for us to receive and use.

It has become fashionable to emphasize the story of Jesus as the centre of the power of the Christian message, as distinct from concepts and doctrines. In so far as it is suggested that attention to the story was the way of the first Christians, then plainly it is far from being the whole truth. The first Christian writer, Paul, may indeed have held to the story, but it was, for all we can tell, in its barest form and denuded of all narrative power. Paul was firmly a man of doctrine. Yet modern New Testament study is right to emphasize the power of the story of Jesus for many early Christians.[30] It was what they were presented with and nourished by. The story of Jesus, or rather, we have to say once more, the stories of Jesus – for we cannot penetrate behind the variety of ways in which his story was told and he was regarded. Yet, despite the variety, there is unity in the *fact* of the story, so that Christian theology then had this fertile, imaginative quality, this inescapable potentiality for growth and movement. Much of that potentiality was stunted or wasted as conceptuality, doctrine, came to predominate in the Hellenistic church; some of it ran to seed in gnostic myth-making. Still, attentiveness to the story is a permanent offering from the New Testament to the Church and from New Testament scholarship to doctrine. It has the importance of indicating that doctrine should not, if undertaken in its traditional ways and according to its conventional understanding of itself, rule the roost in Christian endeavour but take its place within the rich variety constituted by prayer, liturgy, ethics and common Christian life. In all these spheres, the story of Jesus will continue to exercise its non-directive, open power, ready to give rise to new and unforeseeable effects. New Testament theology's happiest and central task may be simply to present the story as honestly and vividly as it can, hoping that Christians will absorb the lessons of its mode as well as its content.

In sum, New Testament studies have the opportunity to set the doctrinal enterprise in a new light and to invite a reassessment of its nature. The result may at first sight be felt to be a reduction in the scope and importance of that enterprise. Certainly, it may more easily, yet surely advantageously, merge with other kinds of Christian discourse: apologetics, ethics, spirituality. The fluidity and even anarchy we noted at the start may be increased, but the hope is that this will be in the interests of the accessibility of the gospel.[31]

NOTES

1. For an account of New Testament theology as a subject, see 'New Testament Theology' by John Ziesler in Alan Richardson and John Bowden, eds., *A New Dictionary of Christian Theology* (London 1983); R. Morgan, *The Nature of New Testament Theology* (London 1973); W. G. Kümmel, *The New Testament: the History of the Investigation of its Problems* (London 1973); L. Goppelt, *Theology*

of the New Testament I (Grand Rapids 1981), pp. 251–81; R. Morgan with J. Barton, *Biblical Interpretation* (Oxford, 1988).

2. For example, R. Bultmann's *Theology of the New Testament* (London 1952), takes a historical and descriptive path but is imbued with firm doctrinal purpose of a Lutheran–existentialist kind.

3. Such a programme determines the analysis given in H. Ridderbos, *Paul, an Outline of his Theology* (London 1975), but starting from a New Testament point of view. For an example of a dogmatic theologian turning to the New Testament for texts and topics, it is instructive to reflect on the procedure in a work like J. Macquarrie, *Principles of Christian Theology* (London 1966); for instance, the treatment of angels, pp. 215–18.

4. Thus, doctrinal positions and credal assertions about the Holy Spirit were arrived at in the fourth century on the basis of New Testament texts (for example, 'Lord' in the Nicene Creed, cf. 2 Corinthians 3.17), whose original sense is now seen to be quite other, as they are viewed within their first-century setting and in the context of the thought of the particular New Testament writer. See J. N. D. Kelly, *Early Christian Creeds* (London 1950), pp. 338ff.

5. As in the case of a writer like Hegel whose starting-point is a frankly philosophical framework.

6. For example, the work of Maurice Wiles, especially *Faith and the Mystery of God* (London 1982), and the earlier *What is Theology?* (London 1976); and Schubert Ogden (for example, *The Point of Christology* [London 1982]).

7. Such as: why attend to this first-century literature anyway? Why attach importance to Jesus' self-understanding or opinions?

8. This has been a major factor in the demise of the biblical theology fashionable a generation ago; see 'Biblical Theology' by J. L. Houlden, in Alan Richardson and John Bowden, ed., *A New Dictionary of Christian Theology* (London 1983); James Barr, *The Bible in the Modern World* (London 1973): ibid., *Explorations in Theology 7* (London 1980).

9. Often seen as a weakness, brought to the surface by increased historical sensitivity, in the work of R. Bultmann; especially *Jesus Christ and Mythology* (London 1960).

10. From the Platonism of the patristic period onwards.

11. Recent structuralist studies of parts of the New Testament are in mind (for example, essays in Xavier Léon-Dufour, *Les Miracles de Jésus selon le Nouveau Testament* [Paris 1977]). In another mode, see also the work of Northrop Frye, for example, *The Great Code* (London 1982), treating the Bible as a literary whole.

12. See C. E. Gunton, *Yesterday and Today* (London 1983), for an optimistic view (which many New Testament scholars would not share) of the essential presence of classical Christology in the New Testament or at any rate of the high degree of continuity between the two.

13. See J. L. Houlden, *Ethics and the New Testament* (London 1973), ch. 1.
14. This paragraph is an assertive statement representing a whole world of modern New Testament scholarship: see J. Rohde, *Rediscovering the Teaching of the Evangelists* (London 1968); E. Best, *Mark, the Gospel as Story* (Edinburgh 1983); W. Kelber, *The Oral and the Written Gospel* (Philadelphia 1983); J. D. G. Dunn, *Unity and Diversity in the New Testament* (London 1977).
15. For an example of a thorough and balanced approach to this aspect, see B. Lindars, *Jesus Son of Man* (London 1983).
16. For a discussion of this question, see the work of D. E. Nineham, especially *The Use and Abuse of the Bible* (London 1976), and *Explorations in Theology 1* (London 1977).
17. The powerful message of Albert Schweitzer in *The Quest of the Historical Jesus* (London 1910).
18. Schillebeeckx's approach is described chiefly in parts one and four of *Christ* (London 1980), and in his *Interim Report on the Books Jesus and Christ* (London 1980).
19. Readers may like to compare S. W. Sykes, *The Identity of Christianity* (London 1984), part three.
20. See Robert Wilken, *The Myth of Christian Beginnings* (London 1979).
21. Contrast the relegation to secondary status by Luther of the Epistle of James, judged by the test of justification by faith; or the contrast between the inferior position given to the Pastoral Epistles by E. Käsemann and others (because of their witness to 'early catholicism') and the weight put upon them by many Anglican theologians (because of their alleged witness to Catholic church order).
22. Contrast essays five and six (by A. E. Harvey and G. Vermes) in A. E. Harvey, ed., *God Incarnate, Story and Belief* (London 1981), for their accounts of the historical role of Jesus as a basis for faith in him.
23. See John Knox, *The Death of Christ* (London 1959), part three.
24. See E. P. Sanders, *Paul and Palestinian Judaism* (London 1977); ibid. *Paul, the Law and the Jewish People* (Philadelphia 1983); H. Räisänen, *Paul and the Law* (Tübingen 1983).
25. See W. Kelber, *The Oral and the Written Gospel* (Philadelphia 1983); E. D. Hirsch, *The Aims of Interpretation* (Chicago 1976).
26. See David Hill, *Greek Words and Hebrew Meanings* (Cambridge 1967).
27. It is instructive to contrast a standard 'plain' history of doctrine such as J. N. D. Kelly, *Early Christian Doctrines* (London 1958), with the understanding of the same period derived from works such as Peter Brown, *Augustine of Hippo* (London 1967), and R. A. Markus, *Christianity in the Roman World* (London 1974). See also J. H. S. Kent, *The End of the Line?* (London 1983).
28. 'Less predictable': note the pressures on a body like the Church of England's Doctrine Commission in recent years to move from

questions of method and the setting of doctrine to questions of content – what is to be believed. It is reflected in the contrast between the two publications, *Christian Believing* (London), and *Believing in the Church* (London), issued in 1976 and 1981.

29. See J. McManners, *Death and the Enlightenment* (Oxford 1981); G. Rowell, *Hell and the Victorians* (Oxford 1974).
30. See E. Best, *Mark, the Gospel as Story* (Edinburgh 1983); A. E. Harvey, ed., *God Incarnate, Story and Belief* (London 1981).
31. This essay was delivered as a paper at the conference of the British section of the Society for New Testament Studies held in Edinburgh in September 1984.

5
The Status of Origins in Christianity

In the two or three decades after the Second World War, greater and more widespread hopes were pinned on Christian origins than for a long time. I do not mean knowledge of them but the role they might play. It was particularly true in what you might call 'churchy' Christian theological circles, which, in Great Britain as elsewhere, still largely dominated the academic theological scene. Academic theologians might be startling sometimes in their historical judgements on some aspect of the Bible or the life of Jesus or early Christian development, but they mostly saw themselves as contributing to the Christian cause and serving the Church. Though more detached study of Christianity as a religion among the religions was well advanced, it was a minority pursuit and had scarcely impinged on the great bulk of theological thought. The study of Christian origins offered hope especially in the ecumenical sphere. It looked as if the disparate sets of beliefs of the developed traditions of Christendom might reach a consensus on an essence of Christianity, such as it had been at the beginning. This suited Protestants very well indeed because it was a thoroughly scriptural way of looking at things, and for a time, around Vatican II, it also suited Catholics who saw in biblical origins a way of renewing faith from the roots. Now a bit marooned, it remains the philosophy behind negotiations such as the long drawn-out proceedings of ARCIC. It had a vital counterpart in the liturgical sphere, where evidence did not permit a return to origins quite, but, for purposes of liturgical reform you went back as far as you could into the patristic period. It was not all plain sailing, even in the heyday of this approach, because the early Christian consensus was not identifiable on all subjects, especially some that mattered a great deal to modern churchmen. Hopes of closing gaps between Anglicans and the Free Churches foundered largely on an inability to agree about which patterns of ministry could be traced back to the beginning.

This appeal to origins has come to seem increasingly problematic in recent years; and it was always open to severe theoretical objections. It has become problematic chiefly because of the growth of awareness of the diversity in early Christianity and of its culture-bound character. As far back as we can go, different groups of Christians believed and expressed their beliefs in different ways, and the differences are traceable to varieties of cultural and social circumstances in the distant Jewish and Graeco-Roman first-century world. The nature of the distinctiveness of Jesus himself remains in many ways elusive, and when he is pinpointed he seems, despite direct, disturbing echoes across the divide, often as alien to us, as unassimilable by us, as Schweitzer noted almost a century ago. These factors make an appeal to origins seem both very difficult (Which bit of origins are you appealing to?) and rather futile (How can we go and live in the first-century world where those origins belong?).

But deeper objections are also present. Origins are in practice the servant of the present. The appeal to beginnings is of course a procedure as widespread and old as could be. Moses 'really' gave the Law even if it arose only in the fourth century BC. Henry VIII thought his claim to independence of Rome much enhanced, even necessarily grounded, by his ability to appeal to descent from King Cole, reputed grandfather of Constantine; and seventeenth-century parliamentarians and common lawyers based much of their claim against the crown on ancient Saxon liberties before the descent of the Norman yoke. All do it, popes, princes, governments, churches. But we know that it is almost totally bogus. Most of it is legend and most of it arises to justify what you are determined to do and believe for your own contemporary reasons. The legend is a comforting invention to bolster present policies. To what extent has the appeal to Christian origins by Christians been dictated by this kind of mostly unconscious manipulation? Well, it is now evident that the Lutheran Paul was created to solve Luther's problems and that the concerns of the historical Paul were of a different kind.[1] It is now evident that when, for example, the Revised Standard Version translates *episkopos* by 'bishop' and *diakonos* by 'deacon', it is failing signally to help us hear what first-century Christians were hearing as they used those words, even if it ministers to modern upholders of the apostolic succession of the threefold ministry. And when it calls Phoebe (Rom. 16.1–2) 'helper' and 'deaconess' rather than 'patroness' and 'agent',[2] it is assisting one side rather than the other in a current dispute where both insist, naturally, on appealing to origins – which have little to offer either of them! The multi-form presentations of Jesus are of course the most striking instance of this phenomenon; and the substantial point is that institutions seem incapable of refraining from myth-making about their past and from living with ever-changing illusions about it.

Christian theologians have been (and are) slow to recognize it, but students of religion have been pointing for two centuries or more to the constantly shifting character of any religious institution, in both beliefs and structure – and this despite formal continuity (e.g. in reciting identical creeds) and firm claims to sameness or (as at the Reformation or the Oxford Movement) to the restoration of sameness after temporary aberration. So the creed is still said, but the way it is 'meant' is bound to change constantly; and it can even come to be no more than a banner of loyalty, carrying no conceptual intelligibility.[3] So too figures called bishops exist across century upon century, but the identity of role and significance may be minimal. All this makes the appeal to origins hard to sustain by ordinary historical criteria.

But why is it in any case so compelling a quest? Is not the upshot of the perceptions of history I have been outlining that the appeal is impossible to substantiate, both in detail and in principle? So why not recognize that Christianity, like any other human phenomenon, wends or lurches its way through history, adapting itself to context, involved in contradictions and inconsistencies, often unconsciously, usually unwillingly, but inevitably, and necessarily if it is to retain convincing force? In so far as there is strength in that last point, then the appeal to origins is the worst policy of any, the short road to ruin. Luckily, as we have seen, the reproducing of origins has usually been inefficient and the present has in effect called the tune. Loisy's statement is apposite here, usually only half-quoted: 'Jesus foretold the kingdom, and it was the Church that came; she came enlarging the form of the gospel, which it was impossible to preserve as it was, as soon as the Passion closed the ministry of Jesus.' Loisy went on: a man's identity 'is not determined by permanent immobility of external forms, but by continuity of existence and consciousness of life through the perpetual transformations which are life's condition and manifestation'. To be identical with the religion of Jesus, the Church 'has no more need to reproduce exactly the forms of the Galilean gospel, than a man has need to preserve at fifty the proportions, features, and manners of life of the day of his birth, in order to be the same individual.'[4] That puts origins in a different light, one that remains positive, at the same time as it disperses their monopoly. What I am not sure about is how far it is effective in banishing the spectre I almost conjured up: of Christianity as like a bus with no visible driver, careering through history; a Christianity with no clear permanent identity, capable of assuming all kinds of colour and shape, even in its mainstream manifestations, despite all claim to the contrary. I seem to exaggerate, but take test after test and the result is disquieting, especially if you think in terms of the Christian phenomenon as a whole, right across the board and from top to bottom, and not of the theologically literate or the leaders alone.

All the same, there must be a persisting unease with this theory of free, random (as it seems) development: whether in a secularized form, i.e. continuities are real, and causes and effects can be traced; or in a religious form, i.e. we can trust God to guide his Church, regardless of whether we can see pattern or rationale – though the bus has no visible driver, it does have a driver! There must be unease at simply putting origins behind us, and I wish to make claims for origins that I do not wish to make for any subsequent stage in the development of Christianity.

Thus, the trinitarian formulations of the fourth and fifth centuries, classics as it turned out, are a response, wholly comprehensible in the light of the times, to considerations live at that period, but transient in their serviceability. They were a reflection, in a specific context, on matters lying behind them, historically and conceptually, supremely the 'event' of Jesus, seen in the light of God. They were not the first such reflections and were not superior to those earlier reflections; nor, unless one takes one of the options offered by hindsight, does it make sense to say they were consistent with the earlier reflections, for changing circumstances mean that issues were posed quite differently and different issues were raised. (Judging the past by the light of developments makes a historian's hair stand on end, though it does not always worry theologians.) So while from the point of view of historical sympathy, those formulations are understandable and even, within their circumstances, laudable, they also contain elements which fly in the face of earlier reflections. Moreover, it is hard to see why the classical formulations should constitute a base line for all later reflection, as if each age must simply build on the whole of what went before: if that were so, there could be no scope for revision or for a Reformation, or indeed for appeals to origins. It is hard to see why 'the' (or 'a') 'doctrine of the Trinity' should be a permanent part of living Christianity. Indeed, outside some styles of technical systematic theology and the official (but fossilized?) formularies, it probably is so no more, for bad reasons as well as good. In this area and in general, exegesis of the documents of origins is the neglected historical conscience of theology, revealing the pedigree of later ideas and resisting apriorism.

But origins are different. Somewhere in that region is to be found that which later reflections are all reflecting upon in their various inconsistent and often strange ways. In that sense, origins are bedrock. But where exactly are origins to be located? When do origins stop? Just as some Christians used to regard the Bible and the first five General Councils as bedrock, others have seen the New Testament and the apostolic age (or some part of it) as occupying that place. Now, however, we are bound to see the New Testament as both diverse and as itself made up of parts of the reflective process, itself looking back to and responding to the elusive Jesus, taking certain views of him and about him. So, notionally or conceptually, it seems that origins had better mean the phenomenon of Jesus; but, practically, we can apprehend him only via early reflections about him and cannot be sure what represents his own input and what does not. There is an impasse here, from which, perhaps only thoughts along Loisy's lines offer escape.

Yet, for the sake of in the first place merely factual authenticity in Christianity, it is impossible not to keep attending to that origin conceptually which is unattainable practically. So I hazard a definition of Christianity, which, as definition, I should be reluctant to elaborate: Christianity is a mode of responding to God by way of the phenomenon of Jesus as his agent for human well-being. But concern with a factual kind of authenticity leads me to say in a number of matters: it would be a pretty strange Christianity which was not concerned with x or y, found in its beginnings: e.g. it would be a pretty strange Christianity which (however impossible it found them) ignored the negative attitudes to wealth and family ties found in the gospel, or had no expectancy of transcendent good, or failed to inculcate a path of suffering as the route to maturity, and a lack of concern with personal advancement and worldly status. The odd thing is that official Christianity fails on most of these counts most of the time, and they flourish only in pockets of society and in bits of our lives and parts of our heads. I suppose then that the role of origins is that of court jester: to exert a permanent critique of whatever Christian beliefs and attitudes emerge at particular times, sometimes, it appears, almost intuitively (Christians just come to take up this cause or that attitude), sometimes by long tortuous paths of development. And the role of the Christian preacher or teacher is, in this regard, to be a paltry mouthpiece of that jester. None of this implies any scorn or rejection of all those reflections on our origin, from those of the New Testament writers onwards. Quite the contrary. But they are, in their various ways and degrees, all relativized by the look and the voice of the jester.

NOTES

1. See K. Stendahl, *Paul among Jews and Gentiles* (London, SCM, 1977); E. P. Sanders, *Paul* (Oxford 1991).
2. See W. A. Meeks, *The First Urban Christians* (Yale 1983), p. 60; but also Ben Witherington III, *Women in the Earliest Churches* (Cambridge 1988), pp. 113f. On *diakonos*, John N. Collins, *Diakonia* (Oxford 1990).
3. See Doctrine Commission of the Church of England, *Christian Believing* (London, SPCK, 1976).
4. See A. R. Vidler, *The Modernist Movement in the Roman Church* (Cambridge 1934), p. 118.

6
A Future for New Testament Studies

A leading systematic theologian, concerned with the clear and effective formulation of Christian theology, recently experienced current New Testament studies at close quarters, and was not impressed. 'If that's how they conduct themselves', came the verdict, 'they will soon be out of business, and it will be their own fault.' His judgement was frank and harsh. Also it was not untypical of the reaction of interested outsiders when they see the craft in action.

The context of his remarks was that of Christian theology as a total enterprise, in which the study of the New Testament has traditionally (though in a multitude of forms) taken a place as of right and assumed a crucial role. It seemed to him that that role could scarcely be played by the kind of academic work he had encountered. The tool was simply the wrong shape for the job. A casual glance at the contents of the technical journals in the subject, demonstrating the 'coal-face' activities of its professional practitioners, shows what he had in mind. There is much concern still with minute questions of word-meaning and historical or literary reconstruction, much striving with questions which have been laboured over exhaustively (one would have thought) for a century and more. Thus, a recent example invites readers to consider, among other comparable subjects, three problems of textual criticism, and the detailed exegesis of half a dozen well-worked passages; most of the list might easily have been identical at the beginning of the century (though *not* a reference to the friendly computer and another to the social structure of early Christian communities).

A survey of essay-collections presented to the Great on retirement – another barometer of the state of a subject – conveys the same impression. Sometimes it looks as if well-known teachers are better at producing reproductions of themselves, people who will faithfully till the same old soil, rather than stimulate creative thought that will advance the subject. It is not surprising that an outside observer should be worried and irritated at a situation which may be construed, in a wider theological perspective, as a dereliction of duty, or, in an academic perspective, as running fast while somehow staying on the same spot.

When friends offer such criticism, more in sorrow than anger, they have a right to a hearing and, if possible, a constructive reply. There is, of course, a tactical (but in some ways fundamental) answer that springs immediately to mind. May it not be the case that the Christian theologian no longer has the right to count on the co-operation of the New Testament scholar in the way that was suggested? Is not the study of the New Testament now (and has it not long been) a discipline in its own right, with its own criteria and procedures, in no way beholden to the requirements of other interests, and entitled to have its academic independence respected? Would not a situation where New Testament studies saw themselves as in some way cast as the supplier of resources to the Christian theologian spell death to the integrity of the subject? One might feel that over long centuries we had seen enough of styles of using the New Testament which made it the lackey of predetermined theological positions, the legitimator of ideas based elsewhere. And if the work of New Testament scholars strikes outsiders as introverted and immobile, let the latter reflect that this is a discipline second to none in its minute attention to intractable problems worth tackling for their own sake, or for the sake of the pursuit of truth, however long and arduous the path.

There is an unfashionably idealistic case to be made along these lines, a standard to be kept flying, even if tattered from pot-shots directed from many quarters, both religious and sternly secular. It is a noble case – or at least, while liberal values survive, there will be those who feel it to be so. But now, undoubtedly, it lacks realism; for after all, who would ever have accorded to the New Testament the quality of scholarly attention and (to be sordidly blunt) financial resources it has received and still receives, if it were not for its place in Christian theology as a comprehensive object of interest and concern? It is not so much the New Testament in itself as the central part it has played in Christianity over twenty centuries that accounts for its continuing academic prominence. As Geza Vermes has repeatedly pointed out, the New Testament writings, once removed from their Christian theological role and pushed back firmly into their period of origin, would take their place as a relatively minor element in the Jewish literature of the time. In terms of academic resources, their study in our secular academies would then become part of the responsibility of a small group of specialists in that area, doubtless competing for a decreasing slice of the cake assigned to those arts subjects which are not reckoned to contribute conspicuously to national prosperity. It is a change of status which New Testament scholars should not lightly or hastily embrace, at the very least on prudential grounds. Survival is not frivolously to be put in jeopardy.

Prudence is not, however, the highest of motives. Despite the theoretical importance of the case just discussed, New Testament scholarship, or at any rate the greater number of those engaged in it, is unlikely in practice to be over-assertive about severing links with theology, even if it is not very good at relating to it convincingly. In the liberal West for the moment, its integrity is not actually under threat from a bullying religious orthodoxy. Where it is not ignored or left to go its own way, it is rather the case that theologians wish, even plead, that it should give them more help. New Testament scholars might indeed do more to indicate ways in which their work in fact affords such help, though not necessarily in plainly palatable form. As often as not, it is likely to provide not so much useful resources for a task already recognized as the raw material for new ways of envisaging the theological task, demanding restructuring on an uncongenial scale. The theologians' impatience with New Testament studies as currently practised may in part conceal an unwillingness to see a new shape to the relationship, one dictated by genuine developments in the subject and profiting from various aspects of its frightening precision about Christian origins and the foundation documents of Christianity. For while it is true that the journals and the essay-collections seem at first sight full of 'the same old stuff', closer examination both of them and of books and doctoral theses appearing in recent years makes abundantly clear not simply the subject's continuing vitality but also its movement in new and intriguing directions. These new forms of work are exciting enough in themselves in their intellectual content, but they also show promise of attracting the interest of non-specialists in the field, both theologians and others.

Some of those 'others' have indeed helped to stimulate work that is in effect interdisciplinary in character.

Thus, structuralist theories in literary criticism have been applied to the Gospels, and sociological perceptions have been brought to bear on almost the whole range of the New Testament writings and the Christian life which they represent. There is every likelihood that the future will see the development of these and other relationships (e.g. with anthropology).

All this means a considerable shift of focus. For most of its recent history, the study of the New Testament has had a twofold character. Much of it has been (or appeared to be) 'scientific', ideologically presuppositionless: that is, it has concerned itself with technical questions of a literary, linguistic or historical character, and its natural affinities have been with comparable studies in the Latin and Greek Classics and Ancient History. But some of its greatest figures have also had strong philosophical and theological concerns, preeminently Rudolf Bultmann with his programme of demythologization. German New Testament scholarship has, with few exceptions, worked within a Lutheran (or, in some cases, Reformed) framework, especially in the interpretation of Paul; and even when rejecting Luther has often perforce accepted the terms of debate he established.

The price paid for both these styles of working has been the isolation of New Testament studies from developments in the humanities, especially of a literary kind, and in the human and social sciences. It is these defects which are now being rectified.

The result is chiefly seen in two quite different movements, which appear at their most contrary in relation to the Gospels. The first is literary in character, and it ranges much more widely than the austere iciness of structuralist analysis. It shows itself chiefly in an awareness of the Gospels as narratives, whose meaning is to be discerned in their flow as sheer texts – with beginnings and endings, internal echoes and links. In its pure form, though it is in part a development of the fruitful redaction criticism of the sixties and seventies, this approach has no interest in the settings and intentions of authors, or in the history and traditions which lie behind the text (and may, in principle, be discernible within it). While it certainly involves the interaction of reader and text, in a kind of duet of narratives or stories (that of the reader and that of the text), there is here an attractive objectivity (for the text alone is that which we have before us) and an absence of hypothetical or inaccessible entities, like the evangelist or the church involved in the writings of the text and in shaping earlier stages of the tradition.

Awareness of the interaction of reader and text opens up a whole sub-department of narrative method. It would be unfair to dismiss it as a 'band-waggon' element in New Testament studies, but it is the case that successive groups, whose self-consciousness has become heightened by a sense of exclusion or oppression, have taken to producing their own 'readings' of the New Testament. So we have black, feminist, and proletarian readings – and no doubt, in a less stereotyped academic scene, the list will grow. At least they are a change from the white, male, and middle-class readings which may be said to have prevailed for long enough! All the same, scholarship will have to develop some criteria for 'listening to' the text 'in itself' rather than using it merely as the sounding-board for this cause or that, however laudable. Otherwise, we have here the makings of a re-run of the constantly changing perception of Jesus (always endowed by the perceiver with the utmost objectivity!), this time applied to the text itself. (A book like Jaroslav Pelikan's *Jesus Through the Centuries* [1985], while curiously lacking in conclusion-drawing, makes the point vividly enough.)

The second and contrary movement aims at an ever

fuller and franker picture of early Christianity in its historical context and as itself the setting for the New Testament writings. Here historical study has achieved both new sharpness of focus and the use of new vantage-points. Negatively, the former has resulted in the elimination of that long-lasting tendency (amounting often to determination) to falsify the Jewish setting of Jesus and the early Church in such a way as to heighten their distinctiveness and give it a character congenial to the modern interpreter (often, it has to be admitted, in his non-academic *persona*, taken, without conscious corruption, to represent 'the way things are'). The work of scholars like E. P. Sanders and Samuel Sandmel has done much to scotch common myths in this area and to identify the distinctiveness more accurately with regard to both Jesus and Paul. It is noteworthy – and, we may hope, a sign for the future – that Jewish and Christian scholars have both worked in this area and succeeded largely in producing 'agreed versions'. Even sensitive matters like the seat of responsibility for Jesus' death have come into this category, as we see in Ellis Rivkin's *What Crucified Jesus?* (1984). We owe this development less to religious initiatives in themselves than to the liberal ethos in American academic life.

The sociological approach of Gerd Theissen, W. A. Meeks and others amounts to a new perspective on early Christian life. On the theoretical side, it owes much to the work of Max Weber and Peter Berger; practically, if has benefited from the growth of inscriptional and other archaeological evidence; but its most conspicuous success has been in providing a convincing picture of the social realities of the early Christian movement, especially in the work of Paul and his associates, drawing attention in a salutary way to the crucial role of meals (who may eat with whom and on what terms?), money (who may pay for whom and with what consequences?), and status, in a period long idealized in the interests of various brands of theology or spirituality.

The effect of these newly-slanted historical studies has been to fortify the sense of 'the pastness of the past' and to quench the zeal of modern interpreters who may wish to argue smoothly and promptly from 'then' to 'now' and to seek present-day applications of the New Testament, whether in doctrine, ethics, or church policy. As the sociological exegetes have it, such people are out to legitimate the present rather than discover the past. It is in this area that New Testament studies today present their most significant (yet uncomfortable) offering to those concerned with the theological enterprise in a more general way or in its other specialist branches. So far the making of the offering has not been in the least assertive (with few exceptions); indeed, so reticent has it been that theologians have tended to take New Testament scholarship to be simply cultivating its own rather conventional and very private garden. Yet the offering is certainly there waiting to be taken up: perhaps, if it carries a message, it asks to be used courageously – for it reckons to be part of relevant truth, not to be dismissed but somehow accommodated, and at any rate welcomed for its character as a gift. At the purely academic level, as these approaches have themselves been the result of new interdisciplinary patterns, involving a variety of secular subjects, it is regrettable if they find it hard to contribute to more domestic interdisciplinary work within theology itself.

The 'narrative' work is scarcely less immediately congenial to theology in general, for its attitude to history, to fact, seems positively casual; and where the New Testament is concerned that is no way to make friends. Undoubtedly, there are here too serious challenges, now of a quite different kind, to traditional theology. And once more, New Testament scholarship might claim commendation for setting an agenda which others should join in tackling. There is promise of much constructive work ahead.

But to return to the field of New Testament scholarship itself. What are likely to be the developments of the future? Like those of the present, they will surely both grow out of trends already established and respond to current pressures in the culture at large. First, with regard to ethos. The signs are that, as far as New Testament work in the universities is concerned, it will, like other branches of the subject, become still more separated from the churches to which it was formerly so closely wedded. This may have the effect of eliminating more traces of the (often unwitting) preference for 'a Christian solution' (already much diminished in New Testament interpretation), especially in relation to first-century Judaism, to the person of Jesus, and to an implicit overestimate of the importance of Christianity in the Graeco-Roman world of the first century. Both Christian and Jewish scholars have in the past frequently erred through partiality of judgement in all these areas. Such changes will, however, create difficulties for the subject when taught by people trained in secular universities but employed in confessional establishments, and teachers will suffer even greater tensions than at present – as indeed will their more discerning pupils.

With regard to new trends in study itself, there is, secondly, likely to be, as already hinted, a growth in the interpretation of the New Testament from an anthropological perspective: how do these writings testify to and illuminate perennial human concerns like time, place, transition from phase to phase in life, and the behaviour of humankind before 'the other'? This extension of the objectifying of the New Testament from yet another standpoint will be salutary if it gives further stimulus to the process of doctrinal re-evaluation and to the assessment of aspects of Christian practice.

Thirdly, it will be surprising if the current interest in spirituality does not come to be more strongly reflected in New Testament studies. There may be a recognition of the New Testament writers less as 'theologians' than as 'spiritual writers', or rather, as examples of diverse spiritual 'paths'. This would be wholly justified in that the tendency hitherto to judge them for their 'theology' undoubtedly expresses the intellectualism of the scholarly fraternity rather than a just appreciation of the New Testament writers themselves, in relation to whom such a distinction is meaningless. Anachronism is our oldest and most persistent enemy!

Fourthly, it would be equally surprising if concern with the relationship between Christianity and other faiths did not find echoes in the reading of the New Testament. Already, as we have seen, historical realities have led to some mutual interaction between Christianity and Judaism in the field. Will there be attempts at an Islamic or Buddhist reading of the New Testament? Could it be intellectually respectable? And what might 'respectable' then mean?

Finally, by way of return to a question discussed earlier: What are the chances of New Testament studies being able to maintain rigorous standards of truthfulness and faithfulness to evidence openly available, and at the same time to make apparent the religious character of the New Testament writings and their role at the fount of a powerful religious tradition, continuing commitment to which is not to be regretted or apologized for but openly welcomed? Many people will continue to want both to study the New Testament with integrity and to give allegiance to its central figure. New Testament scholarship has on the whole been perceived as making the following of that desire something of an obstacle race, though hardy souls have seen it as a salutary process of initiation by ordeal, hopeful and exciting. Apart from the perversity and pride of human nature which resists growth and absolutizes present opinions, is there any reason why New Testament scholarship should not seek to achieve such an aim? Some of the developments envisaged above might assist it. But religion is a corrupter as well as a liberator, and the dangers to common honesty are always formidable. New Testament scholarship will provide its best service if it continues to prefer questions to answers and to admit when the latter are beyond our grasp. But unless, as the saying goes, it comes out of the closet, its influence may scarcely be felt outside its own diminishing ranks; and forces of reaction may well stifle the growth of developments such as those outlined here. All that would be a very great pity.

7
The Development of Meaning

Consider two contrasted ways in which beliefs, policies or plans are communicated to us and apprehended by us. The first is exemplified by the official statement, formal, carefully expressed, designed for presentation and acceptance. Examples are the party manifesto, the government directive, a society's constitution, the dogmatic statement of a church. They are the conclusion of a process of deliberation and discussion, the outward face of decision-making, concealing as well as revealing. In the past, such formulations have enjoyed considerable prestige and been taken in a spirit of relative simplicity and directness. I do not mean that they have been received without disagreement or without people seeing the need to interpret them; rather, that they have generally been taken at face value. If an individual or a body issued a statement of belief, then it could be taken that such was indeed the content of its convictions. There might have to be clarification of the meaning of the text, but there was no doubt that it represented the belief by which those responsible for it were prepared to stand. Moreover, those who received such a statement of belief could be asked to give to it, without quibbling or evasion, something describable as *ex animo* adherence.

An example is the role in English church history of

the Thirty-nine Articles. In the long agonizing story of
their place in English life, attention has centred on the
questions of conscience and of minority rights. Was it
justifiable or realistic to expect all candidates for Anglican orders to give full adherence to every one of those
weighty propositions? – and need difficulty with a
point or two rule you out? And: Was there any sense, in
terms of justice and good educational policy, in
excluding from universities those who could not accept
this particular statement or belief? Those were the
questions that arose, in the latter area in the nineteenth
century, in the former, to a degree, until the other day.
But there is another, quite different, objection which
has played little part in the past but may now impress
more forcibly: puzzlement with the very business of
adherence in itself.

This is far removed from the old difficulty which the
Victorian distinction between subscription and assent
sought, in some measure, to deal with. It is rather:
What can any such act of adherence mean? The problem
arises for those who have been trained into a certain
kind of awareness, which may be described as being
taken behind the scenes. No longer do such people take
documents like the Articles at face value, either
accepting or denying what they teach about the Trinity
or the right of sovereigns to wage war, but they ask
first: Who wrote them and when, in what circumstances, in response to what needs and pressures, after
what process of give and take? And then: What can it
mean for me, so far removed from all those circumstances, and with quite different circumstances of my
own to contend with and respond to, to receive those
formulations? Purposely, I use the word *receive*, for its
generality; for if I cannot subscribe or even assent
(because not only in detail but also in general the
Articles approach Christian belief in a manner and by
an agenda which are alien to me), I might still be free to

appreciate or sympathize with or be moved or influenced by the Articles. And outright rejection will be as irrelevant a response as simple acceptance. Bluntly, what is it to be in the same tradition as those who first issued the Articles and yet to be at such a distance from them; and, further, to be so aware of the process both of their production and of their transmission from 1563 to now through so many vicissitudes of Christian and of English life?

Along these lines there is reason to feel dissatisfaction with that way of expressing and apprehending beliefs and policies which I described. Given our (increasingly common) susceptibility to background, our instinct to ask immediately what lies behind the scenes and to regard what appears on the surface as merely a front for what is really interesting and significant, we can no longer receive statements of belief with the directness and simplicity which our predecessors were able to display.

This dissatisfaction points me towards the second, contrasting way in which beliefs and policies are expressed and apprehended. How do I come to know what a friend means when he speaks to me about his convictions or opinions? It is partly by the words themselves, as they would appear if transcribed on to the printed page. But also I have learnt to know his mind from the tone of his voice, the glance of his eye, the gesture of his hand; and from whatever I have come to know of his history, his education, his achievements and his sufferings. To listen with intent and to be in a position to receive his meaning is ideally to be alert to all that as he speaks. Even if his subject is abstract and quite impersonal, his whole self is the vehicle of his communication.

Among Austin Farrer's sermons is one entitled, almost appropriately (for it was the penultimate sermon of his life), *The Ultimate Hope*.[1] It moves me every time I read it; but more moving still is a recording of him preaching it, six days before his death. There are so many subtleties in the spoken piece which you would never guess from the print. Can it be said that the meaning is different in the two cases? Certainly it can be said that the meaning for me is different. The recording invites me behind the scenes.

Detail affects meaning; it is its symptom and its significant clue. If I am to know what the Creed of Nicaea means, it is not enough to read Oliver Quick on the words and concepts or even J. N. D. Kelly on the evolution of the text.[2] I must discover all I can about the inner and outer lives of those who formed it, about what it felt like to be in their world, to be a Christian bishop so soon after the end of Diocletian's persecution, about the echoes which stirred in you as you uttered *homoousios tō patri*. As they rather precociously incorporated that muddling term (as they soon discovered), what new meaning had they injected into the Christian bloodstream? Had they developed or diverted faith, elucidated it or over-defined it? And what am I supposed to think, as I, having done my best to enter into their world and their imagination, return from that alien place to the patchwork-quilt Christianity of my own day? What would it be for me to share that Nicene faith, and is it a feat I can attempt?

In pursuit of the banal enough hypothesis that detail affects meaning, I turn to a different kind of example before moving to general statement.

In Mark 9.38–41 is the episode usually referred to as 'the strange exorcist'. It contains the saying (v. 40): 'For he who is not against us is for us.' Matthew has no parallel to the episode as a whole, but bits of it appear elsewhere in his Gospel. Mark 9.40 appears at Matt. 12.30 – but in reversed form: 'He that does not gather with me scatters.' Also, Mark 9.41 appears at Matt. 10.42 with what may be only Matthean stylistic changes. To complete the picture, Luke (9.49f.) has a shortened version of the episode of the strange exorcist, including a slightly modified parallel to the saying in Mark 9.40: 'For he that is not against *you* is on *your* side.' Also, a mere couple of chapters later, Luke has an exact parallel to the Matthean saying (Luke 11.23): 'He that is not with me is against me, and he that does not gather with me scatters.'

What are we to make of this state of affairs? There is first the question of the relationship between the various sayings. It is quite possible that I was wrong to see the Matthean saying as in any way related to the Marcan: perhaps it was a Q saying which Matthew used, either simply because he discovered it in his source or because he found it congenial – the latter in any case, because he certainly omitted Mark's saying bearing the contrary sense. Or perhaps he took Mark's saying and reversed it, then incorporated it within another Marcan passage on exorcism, because, in its reversed form, it sharpened the point he wished to make there. That is to say, he disagreed with Mark and was even willing, here as elsewhere, to use Mark's material to make a case quite contrary to Mark's. In fact, the source question makes little difference: whether Matthew was using Mark or Q or creating freely, his teaching is the opposite of Mark's – and that is where our interest lies.

What to make of Luke's inclusion of both doctrines is more difficult still. Whether he was using Mark-plus-Q or Mark-plus-Matthew, it is hard to ascribe to him any more praiseworthy achievement than either plain oversight or giddy indifference to the issue at stake. (He appears not to be in the habit of simply reproducing material without regard to its coherence with his message as a whole.)

What then was that issue? Undoubtedly, that of the attitude to be taken by Jesus' followers to others, who, while not of their professed number, were in some sense supporters or admirers or else seemed to be working in a comparable cause. But where are we to place these sayings and the situation to which they are reactions – in Jesus' lifetime or in the conditions of the churches which produced the three Gospels? It is impossible, short of a dogma on the subject, to be sure of the former; it is, surely, impossible to be uncertain of the latter. And even if the sayings belong to both settings, first one and then the other, my purpose is served; but it is the second which concerns me.

So the evangelists included the sayings at least partly because they reflected their various needs and outlooks. It is not difficult to sketch a scenario for each, or at any rate for Mark and Matthew (Luke may, for the present purpose, be allowed to baffle us). For the sake of my wider aim, I shall paint in broad strokes.

First, Matthew: 'He that is not with me is against me.' It is well known that a great deal in the Gospel of Matthew seems to betray a writer concerned with the discipline and bounds of the Christian community. It is not clear whether his mind stretched to knowledge or grasp of the whole Church or was in practice mostly confined to his own congregation. Certainly his horizon sometimes widens (16.18 and 28.16–20), but perhaps with more vision than knowledge. Not only is he the only evangelist to use the word *ekklēsia* to refer to the congregation, but he gives detailed attention to questions of forgiveness, exclusion, and the rescue of the lapsed, chiefly in ch. 18. Moreover, he seems deliberately to portray the disciples as models for the exercise of leadership as well as ordinary membership within the Church (18.18; 19.28). He is deeply conscious of the Church's position over against hostile outsiders, as the diatribe against the scribes and Pharisees in ch. 23 makes plain.

In this perspective, the saying before us fits perfectly.

Matthew's Christians must take care to separate themselves not only from clear opponents, such as Pharisaic Jews, but also other Christians who are, in the evangelist's view, defective: 'Not everyone that says unto me "Lord, Lord", shall enter the kingdom of heaven, but he that does the will of my father who is in heaven' (7.21). Similarly, there are plausible allies: 'Beware of false prophets who come to you in sheep's clothing but inwardly are ravenous wolves' (7.15). Perhaps they are closer than allies: ecstatic Christians who threaten to draw away the allegiance of Matthew's observant, law-directed Christians; and exorcists, whose activities against the powers of evil seem to put them on the same footing as Jesus and his followers. Such people raise acutely the question of credentials. In fact, nothing less than full adherence to the cause of Jesus, i.e. in Matthew's terms, membership of the authentic community, will suffice, and no half-measures are possible: 'He who is not with me is against me.' You are either in or out.

The Matthean saying is evidence for and symptomatic of a church anxious to define and delimit itself in relation to enemies and ostensible but unwanted friends; sensitive about the principle of orthodoxy; and keen to protect and assert the credentials of Jesus and his true followers. It is a church which presumably has sufficient expectation of a future within this present age to be concerned about its boundaries and membership; though it may be that these interests are compatible with a more urgent sense of the world's coming end than is often suggested.[3]

Mark wrote: 'He who is not against us is for us.' In the section as a whole, there appear to be two main points. First, it reflects an awareness of a chorus of devotion and piety surrounding Jesus and going beyond the circle of his immediate followers. In this respect, attention centres on Jesus, the wholly worthy recipient of such devotion, as much as on the outsiders who show due reverence towards him, whether by exorcizing in his name or being kind (giving a cup of water) to his followers.

The other motif is sterner and closer to a central theological theme in Mark: the struggle between Jesus and the forces of evil. This struggle is so crucial and so intense that no ally is to be refused, even if he does not fully join forces with Jesus. As long as he is not actually opposed to Jesus, like the scribes who in 3.22ff. attribute Jesus' exorcisms to his possession by Beelzebul, he is to be reckoned a supporter. So: ' "Teacher, we saw a man casting out demons in your name, and we forbade him, because he was not following us." But Jesus said, "Do not forbid him; for no one who does a mighty work in my name will be able soon after to speak evil of me. For he that is not against us is for us." '

Viewed more narrowly within its setting in Mark's own church, the passage stands out as evidence for the urgency with which that community saw its task, in this case that aspect of it which involved continuing Jesus' exorcistic work (cf. 3.14f.; 6.7). Negatively, the saying before us also indicates priorities: properly attested church membership is less important, whether because the crisis has been reached or more generally, than engagement in the cause.

Matthew felt unable to swallow that. But then, his total awareness of the shape and atmosphere of the Christian life was different: less seized by crisis, more settled and ordered; less crusading, more observant. So his judgement on this matter also differed. He declined to incorporate Mark's passage, and, as far as the saying was concerned, either adopted its contrary from Q or elsewhere, or boldly reversed it and placed it where it could aid his own purpose.

As a friend's glance gives away a wider range of meaning than his words, and, if I could capture it and examine it, would lead me deep into his whole history and world, so the detail in the Gospels opens a door into the writer's whole perception of things. In the case of our chosen example, the issue at stake is of considerable importance but not in itself central. At first sight, its interest relates chiefly to a practical question in church life: how tightly are the boundaries to be drawn? But we soon found ourselves led in both cases towards deeper issues, in effect some of the great theological interests of the two writers concerned. Can we go further still? Can we say that each of the two sayings is symptomatic of a distinct picture of God and his purposes, derives necessarily from a distinct theology? It would mean that in these two Gospels we are to see not only different portraits of Jesus (we have begun to get used to that) but also different theologies, different world–outlooks. The one, Matthew, sees God as operating in his saving action exclusively through a delimited, observable community, which exercises his power and discipline and determines the application of his energy in the world. For the other, Mark, the cause seems more important than its instrument, the sovereignty of God more vital than the credentials of those who transmit it or manifest it. At all costs, that sovereignty is to be received; and man, even churchman, is its agent not its custodian. Between the two theologies it is not fanciful to see a great gulf which, if not fixed, is hard to bridge. Reformations have been caused by it. The level at which they differ could scarcely be deeper. Can Christianity ultimately contain both?

Before we leave this perhaps by now wearisome example, one other aspect of it is worth our notice. It is the movement, or the fact of the development, from the one Gospel to the other, the one theology to the other. How hard it is to choose between possible interpretations of that movement. Did Matthew disagree with Mark's standpoint and wish to produce a reformed doctrine, but for some reason found it necessary or advisable to use Mark's book as his basis? Or, approving of Mark, did he set out to write an ampler version which would not only give more information, especially about Jesus' teaching, but also bring out the true meaning of Mark as he saw it? If so, then the alterations to Mark, which often seem to us to change Mark's meaning totally, were regarded by him as clarifications. As far as it goes, the instance we have been considering, involving the dropping of a presumably uncongenial Marcan episode, seems to speak for the former hypothesis.

But whichever of the two is closer to the truth (and perhaps we are now incapable of entering so intimately into the thoughts of these men), we witness at this early stage such a creative handling of what we may already call tradition that it produces not just a new judgement on some minor issue but, by implication, a different Christian theology – that is, a different picture of God and his purposes validated by and through Jesus.

It might be felt that the line of argument taken here exaggerates the difference between the two evangelists beyond reason. After all, the Church has lumped them happily together in the New Testament for centuries and has not only seen over divergences such as this but has used the Gospels as part of the backing for a unified theology. A view of things seen by a handful of latter-day, historically sensitive students of the New Testament surely carries little weight.

But certain kinds of truth once seen, certain perspectives once discerned, cannot be obscured. They impose themselves, willy-nilly. Whether a certain way of assessing the past is of long standing or arose yesterday is beside the point: the question is, is it a valid way of looking at the phenomena? In this case, the approach taken to the Gospels, involved in our minor example, is both proper and illuminating. But it is not in the least surprising if it is received with reluctance.

For does it not imply an impossibly slippery quality in Christian theology, almost a frivolity? If we are to go behind the scenes so ruthlessly and follow up hints so sensitively, will not deep gulfs open up everywhere? Will not every mind that applies itself to the question of God, even within an identifiable tradition, hold different views from every other, so that creeds and sonorous agreed statements are, from this unyielding and relentless viewpoint, no more than flimsy bridges beneath which the gulfs still yawn?

It is worth withdrawing from that vertiginous prospect and staring our own reluctance coolly in the face. We should banish all sense of grudge against Matthew for tampering with the tradition he received; subdue our preference for the one evangelist or the other as now unmasked. We should even transcend an emerging readiness to admit that each writer expresses his own special vision.

The further step is to welcome the variety and to see where it leads. Matthew differed from Mark for two underlying reasons. First, he brought to his Christian perception a distinct psychological make-up (largely obscure to us) and a distinct educational formation (clearer to us, from his writing and from our knowledge of contemporary Judaism). Second, he was subject to distinct needs and pressures, some of which we can attempt to identify from the emphases and expression of his writing. Inevitably, these factors formed his work and dictated the way in which he was capable of receiving not only the Gospel of Mark but also Jesus who lay behind Mark and the God whom Jesus mediated. Moreover, lest we should regard Mark as bedrock, what was true of Matthew was also true of him.

The picture of the nature of Christian theology and of its transmission which I have partly presented but largely implied is at first sight daunting and unappetizing. Worse, it is oversimplified and unfair. Clearly, deep distinction does not mean that nothing is held in common. Matthew and Mark confess one Jesus, acknowledge common Scriptures seen to be fulfilled, proclaim one gospel of a Kingdom embodied in Jesus, and in some sense share a single fellowship. However fiercely they might have disputed if forced into one another's company, we, looking back, can see how they were part of a single enterprise in the world of their time and over against other elements within it. Their varied emphases may be seen as complementary contributions to a single overriding task. We can subsume them (and their fellows) within the dynamic process whereby the Christian teaching established itself and applied itself to people of many kinds of cultural background.

Further, the eventual emergence of formal agreed statements of belief at various stages of Christian history is not a negligible factor, left in the air as we become more aware of the welter of individual shades of belief and religious expression. Among the earliest such agreed statements we must indeed place the canon of Scripture, including Matthew and Mark, which, however it dulls the individuality of the voices which make it up, nevertheless has its own intelligible effect. In fact, the agreed statements positively counteract the variety, blunt sharp edges, articulate consensus, and then in their turn help to form the distinctive belief of individuals, as one factor alongside the rest.

So between the two contrasting ways in which beliefs and policies are communicated and apprehended, one might advance a bridging hypothesis. As far as traditional assumptions are concerned, it would involve essentially a redistribution of weight. That picture of Christian life and faith which sees churches (even Christianity) as expressing a single unified pattern of belief, enshrined in formulas, expressed in a transmitted though developing theological structure, must certainly be modified in the face of the considerations, both historical and human, which are now so clear to us. The story is not one of smooth or even jolting development in one clearly identifiable direction. It is also a tale of contradictions, stops and starts. And even apparently solid continuity (as, for example, with regard to the non-ordination of women) is deceptive, for the settings, both social and doctrinal, within which the tradition has existed are immeasurably diverse.

From a quite different consciousness, Eastern Orthodoxy, with its sense of authority for faith embodied not simply in the ecclesiastical magisterium but more pervasively through the whole body of the faithful, represents a view comparable *in certain ways* to that which now emerges. Such a view puts more weight, in the holding and transmission of Christian belief, on the community as a whole and on its members, frankly recognized and appreciated for their necessary diversity and not for their capacity to toe the line. It does not overestimate the place of theology – that is, the orderly, rational statement of belief – among the expressions of Christian life and awareness. It will be more ready than we have often been to encourage new expressions of Christian vitality, in spirituality and moral action, which might be hard to square with certain traditional patterns or statements of belief. It will not expect the same expressions to be everywhere appropriate and valid.

It might seem that, with or without awareness of some of the historical and human factors which I have been trying to recognize, Christian life is now in fact pressing towards such paths as these. There is a sense in which we must simply come to terms with the facts. Their implications in relation to the more offiicial doctrinal activities of the Churches (for example, in ecumenical negotiations and attempts to establish formal agreement between Christian bodies) must surely begin to impose themselves.

NOTES

1. See J. L. Houlden, ed., *Farrer: the Essential Sermons* (London, SPCK, 1991).
2. O. C. Quick, *Doctrines of the Creed*, 1938; J. N. D. Kelly, *Early Christian Creeds* (London, Longmans, 1982).
3. Despite his concern with frontiers in the here and now, Matthew believed that in the coming new age outsiders who had been generous to Christian missionaries would be amply rewarded (10.41–2; 25.31–46). Mark saw the time for welcome as *now*, not *then*; and saw it as based on support for Jesus' cause, not kindness to Christians.

8
Jesus Christ and 'The Word of God'

We are concerned with the genius of two religions, two
ways of speaking of God, receiving him and relating to
him. My plan is to notice certain features of traditional
Christianity, especially concerning the role of Jesus;
then to show how it constantly runs the risk of certain
problematic developments; and finally to contrast these
with certain authentic notes which will provide my
main message.

But I ought first to disclose something of my cast of
mind. Two theological problems continually fascinate
and puzzle me; and whatever I say is bound to be in
some reference to them. First, the nature of Christian
identity: Christian faith has presented itself and been
believed under so many different forms. Orthodoxy
itself (the word begs the question) has adopted any
number of different and even contradictory
standpoints. Sometimes they can be seen as reconcilable when viewed in a wider perspective, but not
always without strain. Where then is identity? What are
the criteria for authentic and legitimate Christian development? I cannot believe that Newman's sense of a
gradually and smoothly unfolding truth, implicit from
the start, is other than an over-simplification of the
evidence. Take the relatively 'safe' example of infalli-
bility, over which Newman himself had the deepest

misgivings when it 'developed' into the papal dogma; and notice the recent developments in Vatican II which, in spirit if not in letter, all but negate the assertion of Vatican I. I return with constant glee to Austin Farrer's essay on the subject (*Interpretation and Belief*, p. 160): 'Perhaps the Church may still be called infallible, as the Crown is still called sovereign in England, or as dictatorship is called democracy in East Germany.' But, however disguised, may it be that developments in doctrine, often involving deep shifts and even contradictions, form part of a deeper-laid pattern, so that the identity of Christian faith is discernible across the cultures? That is my question. I should not be happy to think that Christian faith, as it travels through history, free-wheels, going anywhere, anyhow, with only historical continuity to give it a semblance of unity. Nor do I think that it comes to that. But the question remains; and I think that our models for understanding development and readiness to greet it are still imperfect.

My second problem concerns interpretation. What exactly am I doing, and how self-conscious should I be in the doing of it, when I say that Paul or Origen or any other figure of the past meant such and such by what he wrote? What is it precisely to enter into someone else's mind and present its contents to the world? I believe in trying to sharpen the historical awareness as we interpret Paul or John, and I resist treating them as if they were my contemporaries, seeing the world as I see it. Yet how can I avoid intruding myself into the picture as I interpret them? What can I do but intrude diffidently and provisionally, refraining from final judgements? I can only converse with them, as sensitively as I can, making sure that I try to hear their voices through their lips not through mine.

With these aspects of background noted, I turn more strictly to my subject. I shall describe three features of Christian belief – which we may be uncertain how to evaluate. Each of them involves contrast. In certain moods and from certain points of view, the contrasts are no better than confusions. From other points of view, they may seem to involve necessarily, and even fruitfully, complementary elements. You must make your judgement.

My first topic is the propriety of speaking about God at all. It seems absurd to raise the question in relation to a religion as incurably and incessantly verbal as Christianity, but of course there is a constant voice in Christian theology which deters us from speech about God as either a proper or a possible human activity. That voice is inspired by three distinct influences. First, and most deeply in our tradition, by the sense of God's otherness: his ways are not our ways – we cannot comprehend him in our little minds or describe him without dishonouring him: it is the sense of the holy. Second, by the philosophical tradition, nourished from Platonism, which contrasts shadow and reality, and sees God as transcending all conceivable descriptions which, out of our experience of earthly life, we may apply to him. Third, by the contemplative tradition, which finds the authentic approach to God to be marked by silence, attentiveness, and waiting. These three influences flow together to forbid, or at least to set limits to, that speech about God which otherwise seems imperative: for we have a gospel to proclaim, a revelation to communicate. And with *that* realization, speech rushes in. The dam is breached, and who can tell how to control the flow?

It is partly in response to the conviction that speech about God is improper (a conviction going back behind Christian origins to the Old Testament and beyond), and partly as a way of bridging the gap between the two contrasting approaches which I have outlined, that the image of God's word arises. He communicates with us and we receive truth from him – we are not in the dark about him. From one point of view, indeed, he dwells beyond all created light; from another, he illuminates us with the dazzling brilliance of his presence. So – to use our allotted image – we hear his word, and – to take the image further – the word truly expresses his mind. Just as now, by hearing my words, you have an opening into my mind and will, by the end, feel able to sum me up and perhaps describe or categorize me, so by receiving God's communication, by whatever means, we feel able to describe him. But the image of the word retains ambiguity.

I said that it not only expresses the conviction that, despite our hesitation, God gives us truth about himself, but also is a way of bridging the gap between the unknowability and the knowability of God, between silence and speech as our proper response. Words, after all, communicate only in part. My words in this book represent only a partial exposition of me, and in that sense they are even misleading as a presentation of what is in my mind. I am well aware that my book is showing you the shop-window of my mind, and not giving a guided tour of the whole premises. Whatever you may think, the former is, I assure you, by comparison with the latter, tidy, orderly, concentrated on defined objects; it is designed to instruct, to impress and to please; intended to make it possible for you to receive and understand.

So God's 'word' is a presentation of himself which is designed for our reception. We receive not the whole of God's mind, but what he wishes to communicate to us, or, at best, what it is possible for us to receive from him. So much for my first contrast. In drawing attention to the various possibilities latent in the image of God's word, I have noted questions and ambiguities which soon came to the surface in early Christian theology and, in different forms, persist into our own day. We receive God; but can it be all of God? And what could that mean?

My second topic is the status of the idea of 'the word' in Christian theology. Starting from the point of view of religious language and phenomenology, we should no doubt say that 'the word of God' is an image or metaphor or symbol or, in certain contexts, a philosophical term; its function is to express certain convictions about God's outgoingness, his capacity and desire for self-communication. Along those lines, it operates in the Old Testament. But already there, we find elements of movement towards personification: 'For as the rain and the snow come down from heaven . . . so shall my word be that goes forth from my mouth; it shall not return to me empty, but it shall accomplish that which I purpose' (Isa. 55.10f.); the word is seen as a messenger. And in reference to Passover night, in Wisdom of Solomon 18.14f., we read: 'For while gentle silence enveloped all things and night in its swift course was now half-gone, thy all-powerful word leaped from heaven, from the royal throne, into the midst of the land that was doomed.' By the time of Philo, in the first century AD, we have come further still: 'But if there be any as yet unfit to be called a son of God, let him press to take his place under God's first-born, the word, who holds the eldership among the angels' (*Conf.* 146). No wonder some early Christians thought Philo had been a Christian bishop and revered him.

While not ceasing to exploit 'the word' as an image of God's 'speech' and sometimes using it as a term of quasi-philosophy, Christian theology, impelled by the Fourth Gospel, opted to take it above all as a term for Christ. 'The word' became a person. Yet consider the implications of that change and of the co-existence of the two modes of its use. I shall beg questions and show prejudice by dividing those implications into negative and positive.

First, the negative side. When 'the word' may be an image for God's communication and may be a title for

Jesus of Nazareth, there is a risk of fusion (and confusion). For God's communication beyond himself is a matter of his constant character from the very first act of creation itself. Is there then not a danger (I boldly call it that) of seeing the person Jesus as the agent of creation? – he is the word through whom all things were made. And is it correct or intelligible to speak as if the world's creation were an early episode in his biography, alongside and in the same series as his ministry and crucifixion? Or is this a hopeless confusion of the historical and the mythological, for which the personifying of 'the word' in Judaism only too effectively blazed the trail? And did the Fourth Gospel, in its brilliant stroke of poetry ('the word was made flesh'), leave too hard a legacy for a Church of more prosaic system-builders and inference-takers?

Put it another way: leave aside for the moment the question of Jesus. If we are told that in Judaism they thought of God's communication in terms of his uttering his word and that sometimes they personified this idea and sometimes did not, we say that they were using an expressive and helpful image. We do not look on it as literal truth. It is an image which could be replaced by others: God shines his light, radiates his heat, unfolds his plan, lays bare his arm. But when 'the word' is used as a title of Jesus, yet still applied to the pre-Jesus activity of God, the way is open for pressing the image into quasi-historical statements about Jesus, only now concerning his life-story before his entry into the world. It is the gateway to the problematic doctrine of the pre-existence of Christ. And it makes us speak of the divine and the heavenly as if it were a plain extension of this world of time and space. That is, to my mind, a pity, because perhaps the root conviction of the Fourth Gospel was simply that God was expressing himself consistently and within a single frame of reference both in creation and, wonder of wonders, in

Jesus the Lord. He was writing of God and his faith in him, not providing a peculiarly speculative brand of biography.

There is one other negative factor. To confuse 'the word' as image and 'the word' as Jesus means losing a certain freedom with the image. As long as you are sure that it is a construct of the imagination, reflecting on God's activity towards us, or, more rigorously, sometimes a term in a scheme of philosophy, it can be an instrument for speculative thought about the being and activity of God. But once you identify it with Jesus, you have lost certain legitimate possibilities: once more, thought has been confused with history, when the two levels need to be kept distinct. The patristic theologians failed on that score – and we still find it heavy going when we try to unravel their tangle.

But there is also a positive side. When the Fourth Evangelist took the crucial step of identifying Jesus not only as God's Son but also as his 'word', he pointed theology in a decisively new direction, and still we hesitate to follow the path as far as it must lead.

Images have both potentialities and limitations. The image of 'the word' of God, in its original form, points to a certain style of religion, of which Judaism and Islam are both examples. It is a religious style concerned with words, laws and definitions. But once 'the word' has been identified with a person, Jesus, a quite different style of religion is indicated; and the question is whether you can reasonably mix the two.[1]

God's word is Jesus: to what style of religion does that point? It means that we relate to God as person to person; as unfathomable beings to Unfathomable Being. It points to a way of relating to God which goes far beyond concepts and laws, but which is always ready for further exploration, for the unintended and the unexpected; for bringing into play the whole dangerous dynamic of love. Persons cannot be grasped,

113

cannot be fathomed; nor can God, nor can Jesus. But persons also invite the attempt, if love is given. So God does to us in Jesus. What Jesus as 'the word' shows is that this is the character of God and should be the character of Christian faith. Mere speech is too limited an image to convey the character of what God desires of us and what he wishes to give to us; not only too limited, but misleading.

That brings me to my third feature of Christian theology. It requires much briefer treatment and leads into my conclusion. It is the contrast between fixity and development in the history of Christian thought. Church authorities and Christian opinion tend to stress the fact of and the need for continuity in faith across the centuries: we do and should believe what our fathers believed. But the evidence discloses not only continuity but also discontinuity; shifts, developments and contradictions, even within main-stream Christianity. The practical question is, what should be our attitude to such development? Is it in principle to be resisted or, even if it could possibly be effective, should such resistance be regarded as a mistake? Should we rather in principle expect development (and even greet it), and concentrate our attention on its proper criteria and conditions? The question is, I take it, how God, by Jesus the word, may in our circumstances be made intelligible and be accepted and known. Our failure often comes from not daring to take the measure of the personalness of the word and from pressing God's communication back continually to the more manageable and safer level of words: formulas, principles, doctrines, rules, including the Bible in reference to which the image of God's word has, in ordinary Christian speech, significantly found its chief use. So we abandon our Christian freedom and lose our power of effective speech, as well as smothering the distinctive quality of our faith. If God's word is personal, then his speech turns to conversation: he wills the interaction of love – where there must always be openness and movement, secure only in the fact of the love.

There is in all Christian witness a hesitation between speech and silence. To speak is to open yourself not only to understanding, but also to misunderstanding; to write is worse, you run the risk of being fossilized. It was, in a sense, a dangerous moment when an evangelist first attempted to set down in fixed words an account of Jesus. There was the risk that witness would be narrowed and restricted. It is a great providence that Jesus himself wrote nothing: instead, he made his impact and set up reverberations which each of us in our own setting is free to receive, provided we do it with persistent contemplative attention to the loving, suffering God who creates and gives everything. The obscurity of Jesus is, paradoxically, the condition of his being God's word to us all.

NOTE

1. It is not suggested that Judaism and Islam lack a sense of the personal in relationship with God. It is a matter of the implications of images.

9
New Liturgies: Worship, Bible and Belief

It is a rather reprehensible way of looking at the business of liturgy-making, but I wish to report that in all my time on the Church of England's Liturgical Commission, in the sixties and seventies, I succeeded in winning only one vote. It was in the matter of the acclamations after the words of institution in the eucharistic prayer of the Series Three Communion service in its published draft. Such acclamations were an innovation for us, but they had got into the Roman Catholic service and somebody proposed taking them over. I suggested altering the last acclamation, 'Christ will come again', and substituting: 'In Christ shall all be made alive'. The words were scriptural, more literally scriptural than those they would replace, and they spoke attractively of the Christian hope in relation to the present, including the eucharistic act itself. For those reasons, I imagine, I got away with it.

However, unless I mistake them, my colleagues did not know the extent of my guile. For my aim had been to replace a piece of highly debatable and unhelpful eschatological shorthand with something more intelligible and credible as a statement of Christian faith.

Moreover, I was striking a blow for the then prevailing biblical theology which saw purely futurist eschatology as a misleading expression of Christian faith in its earliest days. The unsatisfactory character of those acclamations which I partly amended has been widely noted since: the way they move, without so much as a by your leave, from historical statement to faith statement and then on to what may seem speculation. However you categorize them, the three statements (Christ has died – Christ is risen – Christ will come again) represent different modes of speech and belief, and their bald juxtaposition jars on the thoughtful reader or hearer. It is not surprising that alternative forms, which avoid this crudity, have now come fairly widely into use, chiefly from more recent Roman Catholic usage. In that way, I feel vindicated – and indeed improved upon, for the newer forms are much better than my modest suggestion.

But at the time my little victory was short lived. The General Synod, which at that stage of things went through the minutiae of the draft service in full session, with everybody free to pop up about commas and 'ifs' and 'buts', restored the original acclamations which then sailed through serenely into Rite A of the *Alternative Service Book*. I suppose it was a combination of the 'follow the RCs' vote, an understandable grouse that the revision had upset the nice parallelism of the original, and a naive unawareness that bare-faced traditional eschatology was at all problematic. Anyway, alongside 'This is the word of the Lord' as a response to readings, the accepted form of the acclamations was one of the points most speedily and commonly seized on by critics.

It was, however, only an extreme instance of a general and pervasive issue. Many years ago, I wrote an essay[1] (which Ronald Jasper was good enough to welcome, though it undermined much of his way of working – he was a man of generous and open mind) in which I lamented the extraordinary failure of liturgical studies (and so of liturgy-making) to reflect even the elementary deliverances of biblical studies, of doctrinal developments, and of current religious perception. It has been one of the most pernicious practical effects of our conventions of academic specialization. Anyone associated with official liturgical reform over the last thirty or forty years knows that it has rested largely on three principles: the modernizing of language, the recovery of ancient models, and an unreflective biblicism. I think that, with some imaginative exceptions, chiefly at the unofficial level, things have not improved much or moved beyond those principles. Surely they are too narrow for the demands of general intellectual integrity; and surely it is inadequate to tack on the liveliness and thoughtfulness of presentation that mark good modern worship, for, important though they are, they scarcely go to the roots of my lament.

Nevertheless, it is not easy to see *how* liturgy, on paper and in church, should reflect either our present understanding of the Bible or our ways of believing. I propose in the rest of this essay to discuss these two areas in turn, but first I make, rather boldly, a general point that underlies the rest and which is, I hope, controversial. It flies in the face both of Protestant tradition and of much recent Catholic revision of liturgy.

The thesis is that it is time to give up the perception of religious services as having a didactic function. As they can in practice be structured, in a sequence of diverse episodes, they are simply inadequate for that purpose, and having it in mind simply clouds the issue and blurs vision. Of course I do not mean that people should not 'learn', 'be educated', through their engaging in worship. I mean that the kind of learning or education which is properly derived from worship is not of a directly informative or instructional kind: it is a formation of the whole person in orientation and allegiance, a clarifying of goals and priorities in life, and a restoring of creating of vision, centring on God but spreading to personal and societal relationships and responsibilities. So I mean that though liturgy needs to be written and worship planned and conducted with this formative purpose most deliberately in mind, nevertheless even this end is secondary to worship's Godward concern and role. A way of expressing this is to say that liturgy's primary affinity is with spirituality rather than, for example, Bible study, doctrine or ethics; though from another point of view, that of practical pastoral responsibility, the ills attendant on the separation of any of these areas in Christian life are all too apparent.

I have just put my point so positively that perhaps it would be hard to dissent from it, and you may wonder when my promise to be controversial is going to be kept. It may happen as I turn to the negative implications. We should give up the perception of religious services as having a didactic or pedagogical function. That means that we should renounce the pretence that reading brief passages from the Bible somehow keeps alive a knowledge or understanding of Scripture; or that some good has been done for Christian instruction by hearing de-contextualized biblical scraps; or that to make the liturgy itself more or less a catena of biblical phrases inculcates a biblical faith. The Bible unexplained, uninterpreted, as it were arbitrarily extracted, is the Bible misunderstood, or, more probably, the Bible that passes us by, so that it may as well not have been.

But then there is the sermon. Surely there the deficiencies which I have listed can be remedied and all made plain. That is both illusory and, in terms of my main point, misguided. It is illusory because the brief sermon of our day is hopelessly insufficient to the task. How can one explain all that needs to be explained? And in any case who wants it explained, at any rate at that point? In practice, the sermon has, like worship itself, degenerated all too often into a species of entertainment (so strong is the influence of television), and it is certainly unfitted to be at all efficient as a species of lecture except in the most special circumstances. It is misguided to cast the sermon in this elucidatory role because that would distract us from the Godward direction of liturgy and its affinity with spirituality. The skill of the sense of God is so weak in our culture, including our religious culture, that in the brief periods which people now devote to worship we can afford no let-up in that skill's insistent exercise. The sermon itself, assuming its presence, needs to be seen as contributing to that task. It should be a piece of deliberate rhetorical artistry, designed by hook or crook to further the overarching liturgical purpose.

Now all this flies in the face of much conventional liturgical theory and good practice: for example, the notion of the liturgy of the word balancing that of the sacrament; the notion of the liturgical sermon, even seen as desirable at every Eucharist, which explicates the lections of their alleged theme – a style of sermon which now monopolizes Roman Catholic preaching; and the course of sermons aiming to give sustained instruction in some matter or other. This last does at least have more claim to pedagogic thoroughness, but, except in special places, it is still open to objection, both on my general conceptual ground and on the practical ground that the sermon is willy-nilly swamped by what follows and rarely leaves much impression on minds moved on so swiftly to other matters in the service. For that reason alone, there is much to be said for the sermon surrendering itself to the overall purpose of the occasion and recognizing its role in harmony with that. As for informative education for those Christians who want or need it, other provision must be made, and in the plethora of courses up and down the land more is now available surely than ever before.

In making this preliminary, underlying point, I have found myself drawn already towards the first of my two main topics: how liturgy should reflect our present understanding of the Bible. I shall make a number of semi-detached points. Some indicate changes of practice towards which we might work – on the understanding that if the Roman Catholic Church can abandon Latin and the USSR can abandon Communism, nothing is irreformable!

First, the lectionary has become a humbug. It has long ceased to be effective as a medium for scriptural education, and I have just maintained that any modern hopes of reviving that role are misconceived. The Reformation sense of virtue in the Church's public recitation of all Scripture flies in the face of intelligibility and usefulness, as well as the actual, highly selective Christian use of the Bible for doctrine and morals; and even if that recitation, whether relentless or somewhat modified, may be viewed as having a Godward rather than an instructional purpose, it is far too blunt an instrument in enabling liturgy to perform its subordinate function of the general formation of Christians. The uncommented extract from the tight-knit argument of an epistle is largely meaningless, and often misleading – except as, again, the purest act of worship (for which end you may as well chant it, movingly and mysteriously, in Greek). The Old Testament reading, except where there is a plain moral or poetic message echoing across the vast historical and cultural gap, raises so many questions now to which scarcely anyone has satisfactory answers that it is a charade: what is one supposed to do with it? It washes over one: but why choose this form of ablution? It yields some secondary fruit: but the fruit was obtainable elsewhere and unsought in the setting of worship. It amuses by its quaintness, but worship is too precious for wasting on idle frivolity. The role of the Old Testament for Christians, especially of the Torah and the histories, is so complex and problematic a matter that it is preposterous to have it dangled before one's eyes, as if tauntingly, during the course of worship; and it is all the more unpardonable and implicitly patronizing to launch this material on Christians who have little or no equipment to handle it. What could be the point of such an act? It happens of course largely out of inertia and confused deference to tradition or to the authority of Scripture. But this treatment now does Scripture no honour and is much more likely to bring it into contempt. It is true that the use of the responsorial psalm, spiritualizing narrative, effects a measure of rescue; but often at the price of artificiality. Anyway, does the difficulty which it eases really need to be placed in our path?

There is another way in which the lectionary has become a humbug. Its present mode does no justice to our present perception that, to be usefully appreciated, many biblical writings (the Gospels and Epistles for example) must be grasped as wholes; and for that grasping, the modern reader usually needs guidance, needs the attention to be drawn to *these* features and *those*. While it is unthinkable to read a whole Gospel or Epistle in any single service, the point is not thereby invalidated, and we may be prompted to consider the whole matter of the use of Scripture in liturgy in other terms. Suppose, for instance, that we accept the ineffectiveness, in our present conditions, and the outmodedness of the 'liturgy of the word' as an instructional instrument; and suppose we accept that the use of brief extracts is misleading: then we may be freed to use Scripture much more flexibly and profitably

122

in relation to the great end of worship that is God-directed but also forms Christians as whole persons. Scripture would fall into place much more explicitly as one resource alongside others for the skilled art of that formation. That is the true art of the modern liturgist, at least in his or her role as what one may prosily call liturgy-manager or -arranger.

My second comment concerns interpretation. In 1990, Richard Coggins and I published a *Dictionary of Biblical Interpretation*.[2] We cannot claim that the idea of the project was ours, but we think we *can* claim that it is the first dictionary of its kind – that is, not a conventional Bible dictionary that tells you what you want to know about Edom or Pontius Pilate, but a work devoted to the ways in which the Bible in its various parts and aspects has been and is interpreted. This reflects the modern concern with hermeneutics and the growth of work on its assumptions and methods. If any one style of awareness emerges from this work, it is the intensely mobile and dialectical character of the interpretative process. Texts may be more or less static on the page, but the moment they are read a conversation ensues between the text on the one hand and the reader or hearer on the other, in the course of which meaning arises. It is not, therefore, as if the hearer is a blank page on to which the text's message is imprinted, an empty unformed mind ready to be formed or filled by the word. Rather, the hearer enters, as it were, into conversation with the text – asks this question of it rather than that, is moved by it in this direction rather than that. If the hearer or reader is so minded, he or she may ask rather technical questions of the text: about aspects of the author's intention or its original context, or about the structure and formation of the text; but even so, what is involved is the reader's perception of these things, and another reader will speak and hear differently.

Conversation involving contribution from both sides is of the essence of the process.

Perception of this kind needs to be brought to the role of Scripture in liturgy. It underlines in a positive way the futility of the blank reading of Scripture, e.g. of obscure or alien Old Testament passages (but not them alone), where no 'conversation' can arise because there is no point at which the hearer or reader can engage with the text, all the more so if it is presented naked and unadorned. Such reading is the purest ritualism, in the most pejorative sense of that term. Scripture has to be so used (and the liturgy-manager must so act) as to elicit the most intelligent and significant conversation possible in the given circumstances. In such contexts, we grow accustomed to a variety of 'readings' of Scripture, for each setting produces its own conversation; and we may have to think long and hard about the possible boundaries in this unstoppable and ever-flowing process. But two things are certain: boundaries cannot be created by using Scripture in such a way that it is impenetrable and resists all 'conversation'; and they cannot be created in advance by overarching authority, like an old-fashioned parent prescribing what one may and may not say to a formidable visiting aunt.

An approach to Scripture as narrative, which is akin to the matters I have just discussed, pushes us further. The hearer or reader of Scripture must have some point of attachment, made possible by subject matter or presentation or explanation; then the conversation will arise, or (to shift the metaphor) the reader's story will intertwine with the story implicit in the text (whether its context or its background or its resonances) – and both stories will thereby be advanced in some way. The text will have acquired this new, hitherto unknown reaction, and so its interpretative treasury will be enriched, by much or little; and the reader will have been taken along the path of Christian discipleship, again by much or little. Once more, it is the function of liturgy to make the most of the encounter and not to render it impotent, as mostly we are content to do, in deference to traditions of narrow liturgical propriety. In the most practical terms, one lection will often be enough, whatever the past did and the rubric now says; and let it be reflected on so as to enhance its role for Christian formation, or left in silence to work its will.

I turn now to ways in which liturgy might now reflect our ways of believing or even the content of belief. Notice that I do not refer to the academic discipline of systematic theology (as a counterpart to biblical studies) but to phenomena which are looser and more wide-ranging. The reason is partly that I am aware of moving outside my professional field and trespassing on other people's – the guilds are potent among us! It is also partly that because of my Christian allegiance I cannot but attend to Christian believing and Christian beliefs, and cannot but attempt to form a mind on them; but I do it from a standpoint marked by the historical and literary attitudes that make the Bible comprehensible to me, and indeed by a perspective which is in general historical – a sense of ideas not abstract but inside contextualized heads!

It is not surprising then that some of the points I have made about the contribution modern biblical perspectives might offer to liturgical studies also have a bearing in relation to doctrinal ideas. But there is immediately something of a dilemma in this area which does not occur with the same force in relation to Scripture.

Traditionally, and with great institutional strength in the case of the Anglican *Book of Common Prayer*, liturgies have been seen as embodiments of the Church's belief; not perhaps with the specificity of creeds or conciliar canons and decrees, but clearly and definitely so, all the same. Nobody has felt that liturgy might be left free to express beliefs contrary to or different from the

Church's faith, even though the historian can see that such beliefs have sometimes survived in liturgy, to be either overlooked or interpreted in the light of more recent orthodoxy. Nor have many people said until recently that the idiom of liturgy is one thing, perhaps akin to poetry, and the idiom of doctrinal statement is another, more like prose, demanding different standards of exactitude and dependability, and each is to be judged on its own terms. The presence of creeds in liturgy clouds the issue, but one responds by recognizing that the same credal words can figure differently, 'mean' different things, in different contexts of use. A person baffled or even alienated by a credal statement in the study may recite or, even better, sing it with committed gusto in the flow of worship. Even then, liturgy still appears as an embodiment, albeit in its own idiom, of the Church's faith.

There is a great deal to be said for having liturgy perform that stabilizing role. Churches think that they need institutions of stability so that people can see what they stand for; and liturgy is about the best candidate for the task, in terms of public availability and richness of content – especially when other candidates like clergy and synods seem to be at sixes and sevens, when Scripture seems inchoate and controversial, and when articles and creeds seem esoteric. Liturgy then looks like the best doctrinal rock in a sea of uncertainty, and it had better stick to its post.

All the same, there is a measure of illusion in this picture of things. It is true that liturgies may serve as a brake on vagaries of belief, but there are many other such brakes, above all people's innate conservatism, in matters of religion quite as much as in other areas. But here too there is illusion, for people's beliefs and churches' beliefs change more than they recognize as the cultural context changes, and no amount of fixed liturgy can hold the waves at bay. It is not so much a matter of beliefs which will be subscribed to or denied, but of ways of believing, priorities among beliefs, beliefs that are alive and truly count in terms of imaginative vitality and moral action. Then liturgy may or may not change (in form or wording perhaps not by one jot), but it will constantly be viewed through fresh eyes, spoken with fresh lips, heard with fresh ears. Ten years from its issuing, feminist consciousness has already affected the *ASB* to the point of its being combed for error. Usually the changes happen without comment. People just mean different things by the words they use, or, where they have come to mean less than they did (cf. overdoses of royalist petitions in BCP), they let them flow harmlessly past, until the priest himself caves in and says them no more. The 1928 Anglican book, in relation to that of 1662, and indeed the latter in relation to its predecessor, was a monument to such shifts and shuffles of belief. In this way, the *lex credendi* has its way, whatever the *lex orandi* may be up to – sometimes despite its outward fixity, sometimes dragging it along behind it. In any case, neither liturgy nor belief enjoys any immunity from the flux of human development.

Liturgy should perhaps assert itself more confidently in this matter. I have been speaking as if its place was always in the wake of doctrine; as if its duty was to follow doctrine obediently and as attentively as its own constraints allow. But this is to give too much authority and place to the intellectualism of especially Western Christianity. The assumption is that Christian belief is most properly expressed in formal theological statement, to which other expressions, including the liturgical, should conform. George Tyrrell wrote, in an article on 'The Relation of Theology to Devotion' (1899), 'Devotion and religion existed before theology, in the way that art existed before art-criticism; reasoning before logic; speech before grammar.'[3] While there is no

127

ground for a romanticism or even sentimentality which idealizes the beliefs of the less educated, there is value in the growing recognition that the mode of rational argumentation deserves no exclusive honour or even primacy among the appropriate vehicles for the expression of religious belief. Its methods should exercise no tyranny, as if liturgy ought properly to embody beliefs with the same precision and even the same technical language as a conciliar utterance or a work of theology. It is all the worse when liturgy (as behindhand in its perception of doctrinal thinking as of biblical interpretation) binds itself to the terms and thought-forms of classical patristic doctrine as if that were the last word. That is stabilizing with a vengeance! In truth, liturgy has its own proper modes of expressing belief and need be beholden to no others.

For secular analogies, it will look less to the exactness of legal or scientific writings than to the performance of music, of drama or ballet, or to the narration of stories which illuminate, purge and ennoble human experience. From them it will draw inspiration for its most appropriate relationship with Christian belief, its vital part in belief's valid, realistic expression, and belief's development in the present which God has given to us. I guess that without such imaginative widening of its relations with this range of human skill and perception, without, therefore, a frank abandonment of its current canons of propriety, liturgy will lose the power to express and further lively Christian awareness. Once again, our society is so secularized and the skills of Christian sensibility are so attenuated that every chance to form and deepen them, that is, every service that people attend, has to be used with (if I may put it so) maximum efficiency.

A moment ago, I was almost patronizing about popular faith (the beliefs of the less educated, I said) in relation to liturgy. In a democratic age, this seems unpardonable. It also seems unjustified in any realistic perspective: at any given time and place, Christian belief *is*, in practical terms, that which the Christian people believe. True, there is meaning in the expression 'the faith of the Church', though it may be hard to agree on its precise content. Clearly too that faith is not unrelated to that which Christian people believe, though in a particular situation they may diverge, even in important respects – as at present, I think, notably in eschatological and formal trinitarian belief. We are close, once more, to the dilemma posed for liturgy: to exercise its official and stabilizing role, at some cost to intelligibility and accessibility; or else to be in touch with the real beliefs of its participants at the price of failure to express unfashionable, esoteric but perhaps valid Christian truth. Liturgy-makers and liturgy-managers have again to assert their independence of role. They must do much more than follow the popular barometer – considered Christian truth bears upon them as upon other Christian leaders; but they have equal responsibility to convey that truth in their own proper idioms and modes and not those of the makers and managers of doctrinal statements.

The two modes tend, after all, in different directions. Conventionally, doctrinal statement seeks to unify those within its sphere, to establish agreement and conformity, often by drawing boundaries of tolerability. Individuality goes against the grain; creativity is a risky business. But liturgy must provide a net of thought, language and imagery loose enough to catch people in their particularity as well as their commonality. It must be able to welcome diversity of Christian experience and of approaches to faith. I do not say that liturgy should encourage or cater for that chaos of private thoughts which is undoubtedly streaming forth as a concert audience listens to music; but something of the same gentle riot is in progress during worship, and needs to flow towards the central order of the occasion rather than to be suppressed or ignored. Nowadays, we are often quite good at embracing this diversity in the staging of liturgy: I do not know how far it has quite entered the more formal proceedings of the liturgists.

Praying and believing have always interacted with a complexity that defies analysis. There is no way that either scholars or ecclesiastical planners can wholly map that complexity, much less control it or channel it where they would have it go. It is of course possible to grasp something of it by studies of the kind that Peter Brown (e.g. *The Body and Society*)[4] has made of the Christianity of the early centuries, or Charles Radding (*A World Made by Men*)[5] of the early Middle Ages. It is a matter of entering, by using tools from a variety of disciplines, into modes of cognition and sensibility that may be very different from our own. It may be no less difficult to enter into one's own culture, whose air one breathes, in order to assess not only its needs but what it is possible for it to use with realism and profit in its encounters with God in worship. What is apparent is that neither the cult of Christian origins nor mere traditionalism (supposed 'right' ways of arranging things) is any more adequate to the task than mindless and superficial novelty. Those who must consider and even prescribe how Christians should be encouraged to pray have undertaken a discipline whose proper discharge demands skills, knowledge and sympathies of a much wider range than they have often suspected in the past.[6]

NOTES

1. 'Liturgy and her Companions', in R. C. D. Jasper, ed., *The Eucharist Today* (SPCK 1974).
2. London, SCM.
3. See Nicholas Sagovsky, *On God's Side* (Clarendon Press 1990).
4. Faber 1989.
5. University of North Carolina Press 1985.
6. Based on a paper given to the Society for Liturgical Study in August 1990.

10
Doctrine Sociologized

Christian doctrine is problematic today not just with regard to its content but with regard to its whole framework. It is not only a question of whether to believe this or that or how to understand this or that belief, but also a matter of how to see the whole enterprise of believing and of stating what is believed.

At the least dangerous level, the approach may be purely phenomenological. Christian doctrine can be described simply as something that is 'there', present in the world. True, there is then a difficult decision about agendas. Shall we describe doctrine as oficially promulgated, by one church or a number of churches? Shall we describe it in its historical development? Or even attempt the daunting task of describing it as popularly held and understood? To describe it in any of these ways is, whether explicitly or implicitly, to place it alongside other bodies of belief and related phenomena. Also, it almost certainly necessitates adopting a technical and external viewpoint, which might be sociological, anthropological or psychological. Such a viewpoint is bound to be detached from believing itself, and herein lies its weakness from the side of those whose interest in the matter is that of 'faith seeking understanding'. Nowadays, it is hard for anyone setting out to 'look at' doctrine as a whole to avoid some elements of detachment, derived in some way from one of the scientific disciplines referred to or, perhaps more commonly, from historical study; but if he is a believer, doing the job from within, they will not be likely to give him his drive. He will not find the phenomenological approach adequate. He will at most use it as a preparatory or interpretative tool. He will be uneasy if he finds that all he can do is give an account of the substance of his faith as if from outside commitment and the life it gives to him. There will be a sharp disjunction between 'faith itself' and the business of giving an orderly and reasonable account of it.

So, let us suppose that the attempt is to be made somehow from within. The most traditional, and at first sight the most straightforward, approach is then surely that which is best described as credal. The creeds of Christendom most anciently and succinctly embody the agenda of doctrine. Whatever their original functions, they have been used endlessly as the bases of courses of instruction and apologetics. You want to know what Christian teaching is? Then look at the creeds. It is possible to use this agenda with all degrees of sophistication. Generations of Anglican clergy felt not only aided in their work but bolstered in their respectability by having at their side Oliver Quick's *Doctrines of the Creed* (1938).

Yet, quite apart from differences of view between conservatives and liberals in doctrine, defects in this approach have become all too clear. They are no new discovery but they have come to seem more serious. The most obvious one concerns the items of belief to be found in the creeds. On the one hand, they do not contain a comprehensive statement of those matters which many Christians would feel to be important in belief: nothing about, for example, the life and teaching of Jesus, or about the Eucharist. On the other hand, they deal, either in baffling technicality or recondite symbolism, with matters now demanding different treatment. In these categories come the complex language defining the relationship of the Father and the

Son in the Nicene Creed and statements about Christ's sitting on God's right hand or descending into hell.

Behind this discomfort is the more fundamental one that arises from the reflection that the creeds did not arise, or at any rate reach their present form, out of an abstract desire to provide timeless statements of Christian doctrine, but rather to serve specific needs in particular times and places – whether to lay out what this or that congregation in the second or fourth century thought vital for baptismal confession or to weed out false teaching as it had arisen in a specific controversy. It is this time- and culture-relatedness which chiefly renders the creeds unsatisfactory as perpetual bases or route-markers for those keen to weigh up the enterprise of believing as a whole.

Many who have sympathy with the credal approach and others besides would see the Bible as the golden highway to the true statement of Christian doctrine and as providing the framework in which to view the task. But clearly it adds to the defects of the creeds that of inchoateness. A particular church or teacher may see all too plainly what the doctrine of the Bible is, but in a free market there will never be unanimity. Except in the broadest way, the Bible does not lend itself to doctrinal definition, and it contains examples of many kinds of doctrinal working within itself, from the austere, cooled mythology of the author of Genesis 1 to the warm aspiration of the Psalms and the vivid parabolic imagery of the teaching of Jesus. Moreover, there is no chance of undoing the modern awareness of the multifarious contexts of the biblical material or of abolishing the numerous techniques by which the Bible has been studied – despite recent attempts to restore to it literary unity as The Book.[1]

While those who engage professionally in doctrinal enquiry are far from neglecting either the credal or the biblical heritage (and are often inclined to use both in ways that strike others as lacking in historical realism or candour), they often work in practice with a doctrinal agenda which arises from the more mature reflection of the Church or of some part of it. It is an approach which takes its stance not so much at the roots of Christianity (whether viewed historically or doctrinally) but at some point well down in its story – and that point may indeed be the present, seen as the culmination (to date) of that story, at least as far as some major tradition of Christendom is concerned. Such an approach will work with doctrines as given – such as the Trinity, the incarnation, the Spirit, the Christian hope, and (less often now) the Last Things. The task is then, from some chosen point of view, to present the pattern of doctrines, each playing its part in the weave.

Dissatisfaction is here likely to arise chiefly from those of a historical turn of mind, especially if they have applied themselves to Christian origins and to the processes by which beliefs, always in social and cultural settings which are identifiable, came into being and developed along certain lines. Such knowledge, in effect, takes a person 'behind the scenes': he has been let into the secret, so to speak, of how the producer of the opera achieves his effects or how the conjurer makes the lady disappear. Once that has happened, the given doctrinal structure loses precisely its 'givenness' and becomes instead a product – of a particular set of circumstances and developments. Unless there is a massive and selective belief in Providence (which gives special status to the achieved pattern of doctrine), this realization is fatal to this approach to the doctrinal enterprise.

The three approaches 'from within' which have just been outlined all presuppose a basic standpoint of commitment, whatever degree of openness or objectivity is then brought to the task of doctrinal understanding. It seems, however, that just their quality of being 'from within' is, in modern circumstances, the source of their downfall. They are too much 'within' to carry conviction, even to their own practitioners, unless they wilfully (or perhaps innocently) turn a blind eye to all kinds of facts and considerations, chiefly historical but also psychological and sociological, which simply present themselves. There seems to be a need to reach further back into the essence of the doctrinal enterprise, while taking care to avoid the drawbacks of the purely phenomenological approach which, as we saw, precludes real involvement or 'withinness' on the part of the one undertaking the enterprise.

So let us reach further back and start this enquiry over again. We make three preliminary and fundamental points. The first is very simple and radical. It is borne out more and more by modern study of Christian origins in their contemporary setting and it has a healthy straightforwardness in relation to Christian belief in any period. The proposition is that for doctrine to be *Christian* doctrine, the one thing needful is that it should in some way bear upon Jesus, the only really distinctive element in the Christian religion. (Others which seem at first to be distinctive prove either to be derived from him, like the Eucharist, or to owe their Christian form to him, again like the Eucharist or baptism or eschatology, or else to owe any Christian colouring they may have somehow to him, however much they may also owe to surrounding culture or general human religiosity.)

Second, despite this appealing simplicity, which seems to admit abundant fresh air into the doctrinal area, there is a danger of being deceived or lulled into naivety. So the first point demands immediate quali-fication. There is no way of avoiding the selection of some framework of interpretation and intelligibility in which to view Jesus himself and whatever in the way of reflection and belief derives from him or comes to be associated with him.

Third, the need to adopt such a framework is both urgent and striking because some elements in the traditional orbit of Christian belief are intimately associated with the figure of Jesus from the earliest days, and a number of these are precisely elements of belief now found outlandish or problematic. Such are the following: eschatology, resurrection, Jesus' death by crucifixion seen as a victory or a sacrifice, and the doctrinal role of Israel.

If we take up the second of these points, we note that, in practice, statements of doctrine have always involved a marriage of very basic Christian data (the fact of Jesus' life and death) with one idiom of thought or another, some interpretative framework, whether sophisticated or not. That framework has sometimes been historical, sometimes philosophical. For the former, the Apostles' Creed may stand as an unsophisticated example, recent biblical theology as a more elaborate one. For the latter, we may instance on the one hand the Nicene Creed, on the other the developed scholasticism of Aquinas. Whatever it turns out to be, there has to be a framework in which to place Jesus.

Among those now available, general perspectives offered by sociological theory are among the most interesting, the most neglected in theology as done by the churches, and the most promising when it comes to some of the more intractable and frustrating theological problems which eat up attention and energy, seemingly without profit and without relevance to many important Christian concerns.

Traditionally (and this is one reason for its neglect), sociological theory has worked in relation to Christian belief in chiefly negative ways. From Feuerbach and Marx onwards, it has been adopted in the interests of unbelief and has at the very least been, like some other approaches to religion, reductionist in tendency. (Christianity is *nothing but* a projection of human needs, *nothing but* a product of certain social and cultural conditions.) Of course, from the point of view of sociological enquiry itself, it is perfectly legitimate to see religion as an expression of man's alienation or his need to construct for himself an intelligible 'world'. Over the greater part of human history, that need for intelligibility and security has been satisfied by the construction of what Peter Berger so aptly called a 'sacred canopy' – a covering of meaning under which to shelter.[2] It is all too apparent that the widespread loss of such 'canopies' has played a large part in the bewilderment and subjectivity about belief which are now so prevalent especially in Western society. Indeed, the very detachment which enables such sociological theorizing to go on is itself a symptom of that loss.

But sociological theory need not lead to such reductionism: in itself it carries no judgement about the truth or falsehood of religious claims, about the possible reality lying behind and finding expression in religion itself. While (like historical enquiry) it may cast doubt on certain religious claims or create a climate in which certain approaches to religion are likely to look foolish, it is simply in no position to pronounce on the reality of God. Its competence is simply to investigate one important aspect of man's (alleged) apprehension of God and his ways of expressing that apprehension. The way is then open to consider religious reality as entailing truth, from the viewpoint, not now of history or philosophy, but of some of the perspectives of sociological theory. To do this is, in effect, to take such theory 'within' the enclosure of belief (just as historical and philosophical viewpoints have been taken in the past), and then to see what results emerge.

Being Christian, and then going on to engage in the reflective process of Christian doctrine, means, at the least, attending to the figure of Jesus as the one in and through whom God is encountered, glimpsed and served. Such encountering, glimpsing and serving are not naked activities, free of context. Any of us taking part in them sees Jesus in some setting or other and himself stands in some setting or other. In other words, we both stand ourselves and place Jesus (as we encounter and serve God in and through him) in a 'world' of meaning, under a 'canopy' which may now not be very thoroughly 'sacred', for we live in a secularized society, whether we are believers or not, but is nevertheless coloured in this respect or that with sacredness. In other words, the moment we give attention to Jesus, which we may see as the first stirring or the minimum requirement of faith, of being 'within', a socially constructed 'world' begins to be formed.

There is no difficulty in seeing that those who first believed in Jesus, or whose belief in God was now transformed through their attention to him, were bound to see him in ways dictated by their 'world'. It was a world of intelligibility dominated by those realities (as they appeared), issues and perceptions which then prevailed. It was, of course, not a monochrome society, with everybody reproducing the outlook and opinions of his neighbour. On the contrary, it was varied, multifarious and contentious. This was so, even if we think only of Judaism; all the more so if we think of the wider Graeco–Roman world into which Christianity speedily expanded. In that sense, in its own different way, it was as pluralist a society as ours. Nevertheless, there were strong elements of consensus, especially within an entity like Judaism, and there was a strong feeling of the rightness, comprehensiveness and inevitability of one's own particular version of the 'sacred canopy'.

In the case of the first Christians, who came from Judaism and who put their stamp on the beginnings of

Christian doctrinal reflection and indeed, in numerous ways, on all subsequent developments, their 'world' of intelligibility was formed by such matters and entities as Israel, the Jewish Law, eschatology seen in apocalyptic terms and involving categories like resurrection and the Spirit, the liturgical round of sacrifices and festivals, and the multifarious body of observance that made up the experienced reality of Jewish life. It was in terms of such a world that Jesus had of necessity to be interpreted, and to the conditions of such a world that any problems of understanding to which he might give rise would of necessity relate. So it is that we find that a great deal of early Christian intellectual energy was devoted to seeing how the Christian community could be understood in relation to Israel and how its life should relate to the Jewish Law; and perhaps the earliest Christian theological problems of all concerned the relation between the decisiveness of Jesus and the expected End when God's purposes were to be dramatically fulfilled.[3]

Nothing could be plainer than that none of these things form our 'world' at all. In so far as we, supposing we are 'within', people of faith, live under a 'sacred canopy', then it is dominated by none of these matters, and even if we retain some of their words, their sense has certainly been altered and diluted, in that their whole context has utterly disappeared. How then can we at all pretend to live in a theological world made up of them? We can, at the least, claim release from 'Israel' and biblical eschatology as raising problems which are for us to solve. While they may still provoke serious and sobering reflections (concerning, for example, hope and history) which we should be shallow and foolish to reject, their status as problems (in the form that the expected End never came or that the Jews were never converted as Paul foresaw) need worry us not at all. But then how can we in our world of intelligibility receive anything from Jesus? And can what we receive bring such well-being in relation to God that words like 'salvation' suitably come to our lips? That, at any rate, is the right path of thought to take, once we see the force of 'worlds' of intelligibility both existing and changing.

Before answering that question, we should note the absoluteness of the rejection of categories such as those we have just referred to. It is not just that they have lost their immediacy or liveliness in our scheme of things. It is rather that the role they once played has simply vanished. That role related to the vital business of a culture's construction of its social 'world' or structure of plausibility. Such a structure, in order to be effective, must provide a picture of past and future. For Jews of the first century, those two essential parts of their 'world' were largely covered by what we may put under the heading of 'Israel' on the one hand and 'eschatology' on the other. The fundamental reason why these two categories have lost force for us and cannot be allowed to linger in our doctrinal enterprise (except in stimulating reflection obliquely about God's purposiveness in relation to human life) is that they have simply lost their place in our structure of plausibility. True, they can be helped to retain a kind of life by those who seek to live within the Bible's thought–world, but nobody does that with more than a part of himself. He rises from his study of the Apocalypse of John and drives off in his car or operates his word-processor.

In terms of the approach we are taking, we may sense that the very notion of entering upon the doctrinal enterprise entails a hopeful attitude to the discovery of a definite structure of plausibility. In a secularized culture like ours, where many people have little expectation of any very clear structure of this sort, those who are 'within' a field of belief (in the Christian case, who hold at the very least that God is to be encountered and served in and through Jesus) stand out. Sharing the realities of society and culture with those who are thoroughly secularized, they nevertheless determine to set all that within a structure of plausibility in which God (perceived through Jesus) is at the centre. The doctrinal task then resolves itself, in its broadest terms, into the matter of how that conviction about God can be seen to extend itself and carry implications for all major areas of understanding – including, for example, the past and the future, those aspects of reality which, in first-century Jewish life, were understandable under the headings of 'Israel' on the one hand and 'eschatology' on the other.

In such a perspective, we may now list some of the questions which really ought to occupy the centre of the stage in the doctrinal enterprise of Christians living in Western secularized society. We recall that the task is the construction of a structure of plausibility or a world of intelligibility which truly carries conviction for us, that is not simply inherited from another, vanished context of life and understanding, and that does not require an artificial effort of abstraction or withdrawal from the ordinary routines of living and thinking in our society.

For most people, undoubtedly the most pressing question concerns the interpretation of baffling experience, that which makes nonsense of any claim, desire or hunch that the world should function rationally and for people's orderly good. The Christian is one prepared to persist in working at the idea that the best chance of assimilating such experience, where delight is the fragile neighbour of bitterness, lies in attending to the career of Jesus, seen as the one in whom God is to be encountered, glimpsed and served.

In practice, this question is closely allied to a second, that of purpose or end: For what am I made? To what can I look forward? It is the question to which, in first-century Judaism, apocalyptic gave its own, ultimately unsatisfactory, answers. For the Christian, any penetration of this area of reflection and anxiety will again concentrate on the figure of Jesus, whose legacy is to cast the whole matter of ultimate concern with personal goals in a very special and peculiar light, combining deep involvement with a kind of light-hearted indifference or abandonment to God, as in the crucifixion of Jesus. Such, we say, is in the nature of God, and such is the path we can endeavour to follow.

Despite the fragmentariness of modern society (so that it talks desperately and obsessively about 'community'), we live and we believe alongside other people in many kinds of groupings. All of them contribute to the structure which gives sense to our perception of things. It is hard for a church, those with whom one shares one's religious living and thinking, to seem more than one such grouping among many, even though subjectively it may loom very large indeed in the consciousness of some of its members. But however big or small its role for a particular person, its contribution is at least potentially very great indeed in the construction of a person's world. With the possible exception of the state or nationality to which one belongs, it has the best chance of providing a past, a heritage, as well as a country-transcending grouping in the present. What is more, it reaches beyond earthly life itself, giving cosmic depth to the picture with which one lives. But in so doing, it poses a third question, or group of questions; for it forces attention on its relationship with other groupings to which one might belong or which seem analogous to the church itself. In the former category come the family, the country or the political party; in the latter, other churches and religious or ideological bodies. It is in these areas that the doctrinal enterprise, undertaken with the perspectives in view here, faces the question of the Church; and it will not escape attention that in this area, acutely, the range of questions is wholly different from those traditionally associated with theological controversy concerning the Church, especially stemming from the Reformation. That does not, of course, prevent attention being given overwhelmingly to the latter rather than the former cluster of issues.

No group survives long without organization and ritual, and it certainly feels not only more efficient but in every way stronger and more assured for having them. Groups do not always give much thought to making their rituals or customs maximally significant in relation to the convictions and aims of the group, but even when they are relatively trivial in themselves such customs have a way of achieving high esteem and affection. They become precious in themselves and they are inclined to develop 'meaning', even if, on the face of it, they do not have very good reason to do so. Religious groups have every reason to grasp the opportunities given by these facts about the life of human groups in general. They should (and indeed often do) pay the greatest attention to the 'staging' of their rituals and the deployment of their officers with a view to expressing and reinforcing maximally the beliefs that hold them together. In this context, the Church has to give constant attention to its enactment of and comment on the Eucharist in particular, and indeed other acts and occasions when it expresses itself corporately and publicly. It is in this context that the doctrinal enterprise should concern itself with questions of sacraments and ministry. Again, even in the most up-to-date ecumenical work, the agenda is usually quite different. It is derived more from the past than from the present. It goes on wrestling with old questions, which certainly nobody feels strongly enough about, as they once did, to persecute those who believe wrongly; yet it seems impossible simply to let them go. They stay on as a kind of academic or nostalgic debt to the institutional past.

This discussion has been taking as its guiding light a basic but very important piece of sociological theory. Its underlying idea is that the 'world' of our perception is a human construction. We, in our different times and places, form it, as it also forms us. Most human groups have behaved as if their 'world' was simply *the* world; that is, they take it for granted, and act and think as if that world were in no way subject to their influence, their constructive energies. It is important to realize, however, that we are continually at work on this constructive task in a dialectical process, and, once we see that it is open to us, we can engage in it deliberately. We can make it go in salutary rather than harmful directions. All this applies within sub-groups in a society, including those which centre on a 'faith', such as churches. It is with such groups, those made up of people aware of thinking from 'within', that we are concerned.

We have seen that to think of a faith from this angle produces a very different perspective on doctrine from those described at the start of this essay. It is different partly with regard to matters of content, but even more strikingly with regard to proportions. Some subjects simply vanish in significance, others assume central urgency. In the former category may be topics like the validity of sacraments or ministries, the gender of ministers, the programme of events involved in the End of the world, and the technical details of Christology. In the latter category will be questions of theodicy, the relations of the Church with other groups and the conduct of the Church's gatherings for worship – all seen very much in a realistic, present context; and in and behind them all, the central fact of Christian distinctiveness, Jesus, as the fount from which all aspects of Christian understanding flow and to which they are somehow to be related. This determination to relate Christian beliefs as directly as possible to the figure of Jesus involves a reaction against the traditional approach in terms of discrete areas of doctrine (such as Church, ministry, sacraments), each with its own effectively independent agenda and cut off from lively appreciation of crucial parts of the truth about Jesus, especially with regard to his historical reality. Thus, in certain circumstances, the anti-triumphalist Jesus, as he surely was in terms of history, gets forgotten or turned into a doctrinal cipher presiding over a highly triumphalist belief about the Church or the ministry.

A particularly interesting effect of this approach is the way it merges what are otherwise often seen as 'secular' and 'religious' aspects of consciousness. This was apparent when we outlined four questions which ought to occupy the doctrinal enterprise as here envisaged. For example, with regard to the baffling experiences of life, we should feel encouraged to treat them as a whole as we try and think about their significance in the light of God, and not hive off certain aspects of them as susceptible of 'religious' treatment. At a simple level, a sick person who is a believer is sometimes inclined to think of some aspects of his predicament in religious terms: perhaps in terms of possible guilt, or in relation to deeply inward spiritual attitudes of resignation or resistance to evil forces; while he abandons other areas of his situation to the purely 'secular' operations of the medical profession. On the larger scale, the same principles may operate as religious bodies confront situations of war or social injustice. In another way, the same move towards comprehensiveness of approach was apparent in our discussion of ritual, where secular considerations concerning the health of human groups mingled with factors regarded as religious.

The advantages of an approach to the doctrinal enterprise such as we have outlined may be listed as follows. First, to show up certain intractable, age-old and now undeniably rather arcane problems as, frankly, non-problems. They belonged to a 'world', a construction of reality, which is dead beyond recall and into which no amount of talk within some religious ghetto can inject life. The still-born nature of one set of ecumenical negotiations after another about questions dividing various Christian traditions is a prime illustration of this. They are incapable of being assimilated and acted upon in 'real life', because they do not relate to anything that is actually going on in 'real life'.

The second advantage is to concentrate the issue of belief or unbelief, whether to place oneself 'within' or 'outside' with regard to religion within a secularized society, where it should be concentrated; that is, not on adherence to a list of discrete beliefs, but on the question whether one 'sees' God as to be encountered and served in and through Jesus, directly and indirectly, or not. And the third advantage is to show Christian doctrine as precisely not an agenda of beliefs in the traditional sense suggested by formulas such as creeds, but as the working out, in a continual process of reflection, of the implications of the one central insight or conviction relating to Jesus for the rest of one's understanding, that is, in the construction of one's 'world'.

The final advantage is to give a built-in resistance to falling into the snare of absolutizing one's beliefs as presently held, that is, the evil of idolatry. By inculcating a spirit of detachment and a relativizing attitude to belief, the person of faith grows in awareness of God's proper transcendence and 'ungraspability', even though he is in some way 'grasped' through Jesus. At this point, sociological theory even marries up with the deepest spiritual attitudes, matters that are at the very heart of being religious and being Christian, whether in a secularized society or any other.

NOTES

1. e.g. Northrop Frye, *The Great Code* (London, Routledge & Kegan Paul, 1982).
2. See Peter Berger, *The Social Reality of Religion* (Harmondsworth, Penguin, 1973); originally published in America in 1967 under the title *The Sacred Canopy*. This book approaches the status of a classic in relation to the approach outlined in this essay. The approach has been particularly influential and fruitful in New Testament studies in recent years. See Bengt Holmberg, *Sociology and the New Testament* (Minneapolis, Fortress, 1990).
3. See 1 Thess. 4.13–17.

11
Toleration and the New Testament

The Leveller of the 1640s, Richard Overton, justified religious toleration biblically on the grounds that Samson lived peaceably (alas, not permanently so) among the Philistines. I might equally begin a discussion of the bearing of the New Testament on the subject by referring you to Paul's benign colloquy with the Athenians or his un-subversive life in Corinth. But even the most traditional among us would scarcely think that such use of exempla was a helpful approach to my topic, or had any clear relevance to it at all. The first-century situation as it faced Paul is so far away from our modern problems over toleration and his mind so removed from our modern discussions of the issue that the direct appeal to Scripture now seems wholly contrived or irrelevant.

I shall make two distinct probes into the subject, the first an attempt to identify aspects of the environment of early Christianity which involve ideas relating to religious toleration or social realities which may express it; and the second concerned with features of the New Testament which, from a modern academic point of view, prompt reflections on religious toleration as a present-day issue.

I TOLERATION AND THE EARLY CHRISTIAN CONTEXT

Here caution is certainly required in the adoption of a perspective on the subject, and as usual anachronism is the seductive foe. Particularly because the subject is one of continuing relevance, there is almost irresistible pressure to see parallels in the past to present phenomena, to look for the seeds of ideas and policies which bore fruit later, and even to seek guidance in our difficulties. The viewing of the past in the light of its supposed contribution to later development has not been absent from the scholarship of the history of toleration. W. K. Jordan's monumental work of the thirties on *The Development of Religious Toleration in England* (1936 and 1940), for all its great usefulness, suffered from what now seems this defect of vision.

Questions of toleration did not reverberate in seventeenth-century England, when they first pressed severely and openly, in at all the same way that they did in the secular and liberal ethos of the nineteenth and early twentieth centuries. What moved Cromwell and most of his allies was not a sense of toleration as a human right or as a way of enlisting maximum contributions to the constant quest for truth, still less a belief that religious certainty is unattainable or that all religious ideas are more or less haphazard and speculative: it had much more to do with what degree of liberty of conscience might appropriately be permitted and where to draw the line between understandable and allowable error on the one hand and pernicious heresy on the other. While a number of sectarians wanted to go much further than those in power, and some, e.g. the Levellers, did have a theory of a right to liberty in the religious sphere, so long as it was compatible with civil order, what prompted them was often the desire to claim liberty for their own viewpoint, to think their own thoughts without the interference of authorities, rather than a universal doctrine of religious freedom. Indeed most extensions of toleration have been won by the self-concerned struggles of various groups of the excluded rather than broad-minded acts of generosity on the part of authorities. Only much more recently have various kinds of indifferentism come to the fore.

The common depiction of the first-century situation has not been without a comparable distortion, some of it the result of residual Gibbonism: classical society and its arrangements had virtues which barbarous Christianity trod in the mire and enlightened modern man seeks to revive. This over-eagerness to greet kindred spirits should be curbed, and certain quite popular myths about the period should at least be viewed with caution. I refer to three of them.

1. That Greek cities were religious supermarkets, where width in the range of goods was an uncontested plus and new products were always welcome. The evidence is mixed. Socrates was condemned in part for introducing new deities to the city, thereby threatening the civic cohesion of Athens. Some centuries later, it was at Athens that Luke depicts Paul arousing interest for preaching 'foreign divinities' (*xena daimonia*, Acts 17.18). Places and their reputations change but we should beware of putting Luke's picture down to abstract belief in religious toleration, or even indifferentist attitudes; much more likely, Luke depicts the Christian teaching less as a cult than as a philosophical option – and, though *he* knows it is more, he is happy for us to see it so in this setting. Indeed, it is a basic difficulty that we tend to assume that 'religion' in the ancient world meant doctrines and beliefs, whereas it meant almost wholly 'cult' and functioned as civic cement, or, less heavily, as the numinous focus of civic spirit and loyalty.

All the same, foreign *cults* could find new homes; for

example, in trading centres where groups of migrants brought their cults along with them, and, over time, found them accepted; as even Jews, not willing to reciprocate in some aspects of social intercourse, found in a city like Sardis, where, after initial difficulties, they eventually (?c. AD 200) built a huge synagogue in the main street. Perhaps we may say that practical toleration was the result not of theory but of civic confidence, and was in any case not perceived as a matter of permitting outlandish and possibly dangerous ideas but only of harbouring strange cults. Where Judaism and Christianity were concerned, there was here a grave misjudgement of their character, and from time to time that realization brought withdrawal of privileges and attempts at forcible suppression to both communities. Sometimes, what looks like religious intolerance was economic in character, as the silversmiths of Ephesus frankly recognized, as reported in Acts 19.

2.   That Roman religion was equally tolerant, an open embrace offered to all the religions of the subject peoples of the Empire. Here too there is both truth and error. What is true is that cults from the provinces found themselves transplanted to Rome, but it was less of an embrace than a swallowing – a symbol not of welcome but of defeat, and thus one among the battery of instruments of imperial power. Once again, Judaism and Christianity both suffered and benefited from being not neatly identifiable in Roman terms as cults, or, more disparagingly, as 'superstitions'. They suffered for being alien (in one or both senses of the word); and even Judaism enjoyed toleration as a matter of concession and by regular pleading rather than by right or with open consent, and even then there were major setbacks. They benefited, however, from their uncertain status institutionally: Jews were a people (and an ancient one at that) as well as a cult, and their religion was a

'philosophy' as well as a cult. Both their synagogues and, more informally in our period, the Christian gatherings were not unlike many social groups of the time, 'clubs' of all kinds of composition and purpose. As far as the public was concerned, they could merge, harmlessly, into that scenario; or else, in suspicious times, excite hostility as possible dens of particularly exotic brands of sedition.[1]

3. That Judaism was a sort of open forum, an institution-alized perpetual discussion group on the large scale, where a wide range of opinions could be expressed and where orthodoxy remained something always over the horizon. Ellis Rivkin's characterization of the relations between the Jewish sects of Palestine in the time of Jesus by the expression 'live and let live', in his *What Crucified Jesus?*,[2] has helped to substantiate that view, though it does not adequately reflect his book as a whole. It is true that this phrase testifies to the lively diversity and absence of orthodoxy in first-century Judaism, before the failure of the Revolt of AD 66 and, later, the eclipse of the Jewish Platonist tradition of Alexandria. It does not however, do justice to the bitterness of controversy that surrounded the diversity, as a glance at the Qumran scrolls, instead of the rather urbane reports of Josephus, reveals. 'Toleration', with its beneficient modern overtones, is as misleading a term for the Jewish situation of the first century AD as it is for the Common-wealth government of mid-seventeenth-century Eng-land in much of its time, and for something like the same reason: there was diversity, not because it was thought good in itself, but because no one had the power to enforce uniformity. Even Milton was against the toler-ation of papists and the undisciplined religious efferve-scence that bubbled away at the bottom of society.[3]

We must view early Christianity within this context of modified myths. In the first place, the Palestinian movement associated immediately with Jesus himself illustrates what has just been said about the Jewish situation in general and it is in no way exceptional. It survived, in an atmosphere of fierce controversy, as long as it could be seen as concerned with the kinds of issues that divided and stimulated the Jewish sects – chiefly, questions of *halakhah*. It ran into difficulties when it aroused anxiety, for whatever reason, among the holders of economic and political power. Jesus *died*, as John the Baptist had *died* before him, and crowds were to die after him in the overtly religio-political rebellion of AD 66 onwards. To us, it looks as if the will to toleration snapped at a certain point, or else it seems that a line was crossed from the religious sphere, where diversity was allowable, to the political, where it was too dangerous. Neither of these is quite the right way to put it. Nobody in first-century Judaism had a theory about the positive value of the existence of a plurality of voices among them, or saw the different practices of the Pharisees and the men of Qumran as fascinating complementary contributions to the richness of Jewish experience. Nor did the authorities feel that as long as you only squabbled about the Sabbath you were bound to be harmless. On the contrary, any issue might turn into a threat to social stability and thus to established power; and once that move had taken place, authority could afford only a violent response.

There is another side to the matter. In the ancient world the promulgation of a law can never be taken to entail its enforcement, either for long or over a wide area, and a clamp-down on dissidents would not necessarily be pursued vigorously into the ranks of their followers. Disciples of John the Baptist migrated to Ephesus, surviving to tell their tale (Acts 18.24—19.6). According to Acts, disciples of Jesus suffered some attacks from Jews in Jerusalem, but they were far from exterminated; and Paul's more immediate evidence refers only once to persecution at the hands of Jews in Judaea (1 Thess. 2.14) – and it may mean much or little – and no one says anything about further Roman action in the area, until the case of Paul (where Acts does not lend itself to the wholly confident distinguishing of fact from elaboration). Other evidence in the NT and elsewhere, for example the Gospel of Matthew and the *Didache*, suggests that some Christian groups continued to live the peripatetic, charismatic life-style, within a fundamentally Jewish framework of interests and intellectual idiom, in the province of Syria until at least the last years of the century. The Gospels of Matthew and John almost certainly testify to a significant variant on that basic situation, whereby Christianity now lived alongside something increasingly deserving to be described as 'normative Judaism'; though even that is misleading if it is taken to imply that, whereas Judaism had formerly been a cauldron of a number of seething sects, of which Christianity may fairly be seen as one, now Judaism and Christianity are increasingly distinct entities, each more and more clear that the other is distinct from itself. While that may be true as far as many Jews and many Christians were concerned, we are not to suppose that the use had the field to themselves; and in any case neither was as wholly homogeneous as is sometimes suggested. In that sense, both were functioning on a pluriform if not exactly a tolerant religious scene.

The dynamics were different for Christian groups establishing themselves in the cities of the Graeco–Roman world in the middle of the first century. Until the persecution in Rome under Nero, we have no sign of difficulty encountered by Christians in a predominantly pagan environment, and that episode itself may well involve an element of politics related to the Jewish connection. Paul's letters contain no indication that pagans in Corinth had fastened a hostile eye on the

Christian house-groups, despite, one might think, some occasion to do so. For example, the attracting of wives independently of their husbands to the Christian meetings cannot have been wholly welcome (1 Cor. 7.12–16); still less Paul's advice that if the worst came to the worst they could legitimately separate from their marriage partners. Moreover, though Paul's policy about Christian attendance at pagan meals looks liberal to us, especially against a background of Jewish restrictiveness in the matter and in the light of Paul's theological reasoning, the withdrawal of Christian guests at dinner-parties if the temple-taintedness of the main course was revealed may well have seemed ill-mannered rather than high-principled (1 Cor. 10). And even if Paul's eschatologically conditioned understanding of the oneness in Christ of freemen and slaves lacked much in the way of immediate social consequences, knowledge of it, getting about the place, would surely seem far from reassuring, except to slaves (1 Cor. 12.13). Unease about matters such as these may account for the fact that elsewhere Christians did suffer at the hands of neighbours. Apart from 1 Peter and Revelation, and staying within the Pauline corpus, it is attested most clearly for Thessalonica (1 Thess. 2.14), more obscurely for Philippi (Phil. 1.29). All the same, the degree of tolerance is noteworthy. Perhaps the reason lies in factors referred to already. First, the Church did not yet fall into the perceived category of 'new alien cult', but rather of a sort of philosophy, no doubt somehow akin to Judaism, and organizing itself in the acceptable structures of household or *collegium* (club or guild). It is evident that a great deal in Paul's public persona would have led him to be identified as a philosopher in the Cynic mode, and much of his moral teaching would have been wholly in line with that.[4]

Even the more idiosyncratic and potentially offensive aspects of Christian teaching and practice may have been shrugged off in the context of the bizarre little rituals and formulas that might characterize the meetings of a *collegium*. It is of course true that before long the Christian customs were already giving rise, on the contrary, to nasty rumour. And even if the Church may have been perceived sometimes as being a quasi-philosophical group, Pliny at any rate, in the early second century, would scarcely have seen it in such complimentary terms. He calls it a *superstitio*:[5] but then he is very much from the top drawer and the word carries the scornful overtones of 'folk-religion'. In any case, a good many upper-class educated people were coming to be cynical (!) about philosophy as a pursuit: it was mere playing with words. Much of the Church's early anonymity and safety may have been due simply to its having scarcely impinged on the public consciousness. Known and identifiable groups could easily be the objects of jumpy suspicion in the Roman world. Trajan advised Pliny against the establishing of a professional fire-brigade because they sit about all day talking politics and waxing seditious. And by Pliny's time other characteristics of the Christians had come to be known, such as their unwillingness to conform, like good citizens, to the imperial cult. It is interesting that Pliny shows no sign of thinking that they might conceivably shelter under the Jewish umbrella in the matter: by this time, at least as far as Pliny is concerned, the Christians are on their own, to sink or swim in the severely qualified ethos of Roman toleration.

II INTIMATION OF TOLERATION

I now discuss a number of disparate features of the New Testament which have bearing on thought about toleration. Some of them may, in a more or less shadowy way, have contributed to the eventual emergence of a belief in toleration as positively good or valuable,

whether among Christians or among others, though it is
not my concern to trace these possible links; and we all
know that until recently Christianity in its various forms
has been mostly intolerant both of deviant Christians
and of other faiths: pressure for toleration has mostly
been either pragmatic, from minority groups (in Europe,
mostly Christian) concerned for their survival, or philo-
sophically secular in its principal inspiration. Indeed,
one of the puzzles of the modern position is to explain
why many Christians have apostatized so far as to
become advocates of toleration!

The features of the New Testament I shall discuss are
by way of pointers to reflection. They are of various
kinds: some are aspects of the early church situation
looked at in the light of modern modes of study, others
are more the direct product of present-day New
Testament scholarship. In all that follows, we have to
recognize, as has been said, that toleration was not a
subject of debate in the first-century world, except in a
few cases of special pleading for a measure of freedom
by various subject groups, including Jews; we must also
recognize that in the period covered by the New
Testament, it was not a matter which came formally on
the Christians' agenda, whether in a theoretical way or
in making claims for themselves against the oppression
of others (though that was soon to follow). The only
prominent reactions to such oppression were to urge
Christians to be prudent and steadfast, and to assure
them that its perpetrators would get their recompense
when the Great Day came. In the circumstances, that
was a case of this-worldly realism combined with
other-worldly confidence.

1.   The height of boundaries. We return to the Pauline
Corinthian Christian attending the dinner party given
by his or her pagan friend, and consider the implications
of the ensuing behaviour (1 Cor. 10.23–33). On the one

hand, they should overcome any scruples they might have about the principle of accepting such an invitation; perhaps simply continuing the social practice of their pagan days or else acting in the light of instruction in Christian freedom given by Paul. If they were modern sociologists, they would say that they had entered a religious group whose boundaries with the world (at least at this point) were low. Unlike the Jews, whom they probably knew, they were not, in that technical sense, sectarian. At the same time, they may be accused of sailing under false colours. For it is not as if they saw themselves as on an even footing with their pagan friends or, failing the conversion of at least husband or wife, saw a rosy future for them; the reason for the low boundary was that the Christians saw the whole temple cultus as resting on illusion – idols are nothing and the earth is the Lord's (1 Cor. 8; Rom. 14). It might be thought to follow from that that *all* children of Adam are within the purview of salvation as now understood in the light of Christ, and that thought was, almost, entertained (1 Cor. 15.22). However, the low boundary might suddenly grow like Jack's beanstalk and reach to heaven. For if the Christian guest is invited in any way to acquiesce in the host's belief that idols, far from being nothing, are 'something', then it is time to go home. The position is reasonably consistent, even if, from the point of view of the sociological character of the Church, it is baffling. This is a religious community with cosmic horizons, on whose implications it is prepared to act, but not in such a way as to compromise the rigorously monotheistic character of those cosmic horizons.

2.   Openness to the marginalized. It is in a way another example of the same point when we turn to Paul's clear insistence on the admission of non-Jews to the fruits of God's work through the Messiah without their adoption of the key marks of Jewish particularism, sabbath,

circumcision and food-taboos. One notorious instance of high boundaries in the first-century world was being challenged radically, and the essential unity of the human race in Christ and under the creator God was being asserted in outward act. The full rationale of Paul's uncompromising insistence on this point is not, I think, clear. What is clear is his vision of the unification of all divided categories in the human race in relation to Christ – if not now, as far as obvious effects are concerned, then at the End.

Yet we cannot fail to recognize that the Church speedily lost the will to do much to realize the vision in the circumstances of present society or even to keep the vision undimmed. The subordination of women and slaves was soon enjoined as in all serious and orderly social groups of the period. At the same time, this amended and compromising development sometimes had more plain goodness on its side than, short of the End, Paul's aspiration could possibly have: thus, women widowed early in the ancient world and treated as if they were men's equals would have been in the direst straits. Much kinder to subordinate them to men and/or to organize them in guilds for their support and for good works (cf. 1 Tim. 5). All the same, they could have been spared some of the male chauvinist theory. Similarly, to free slaves was not always beneficient: it could throw them unprotected on to the labour market. Secondly, since the making of those arguably necessary adjustments within a few years of Paul's time and possibly before his death, Christians have until very recently failed to do much even to see the lowering of human boundaries as an ideal. Instead they have been prime agents at erecting their own, against others within Christian societies, and against deviant fellow-Christians, often making issues of apparent triviality the occasions of division, as if such division were almost a good in itself, a token of the virtue of orthodoxy of the excluding group.

On the other hand, the preserving of identity exacts its price. The dilemma implicit here surfaces first, in institutional terms, in the schism reflected in 1 John, and is visible too in the Pastoral Epistles and the Revelation of John, all from the end of the first century. In no case do we find anything approaching reflection on the situation as constituting a dilemma, for example between Christian truth and Christian love. The writer in each case simply assumes the correctness of his own perception of truth, and love narrows itself to attachment to like-minded friends.

The dynamics of Jesus' acceptance of ritually and morally marginalized groups, especially within Jewish society, as depicted in the Synoptic Gospels, are similar to what has been described. Unless it is somehow coded, its preservation in the tradition is a challenge to the view that only that which remained directly relevant in the Jesus tradition was recorded by his followers; for there is little sign that by the end of the first century, when the Gospels were written, the churches held their doors wide open for the riff-raff of society. A theologically motivated tolerance of human weakness, possible in the charismatic moment, was not sustainable as a long-term policy.

3. The Synoptic Gospels. The very existence of the first three Gospels takes us interestingly in a different direction. We owe the survival of all three, when the supersession of at least one of them was in many ways more likely, to these chief factors: (a) the distinguished authorship which came to be attached to them and the stories surrounding their composition; (b) the absence in the Church of this time of any other than local machinery for eliminating elements of which you disapproved even if you were aware of them – thus, the writ of the writer of 1 John ran only in Johannine circles; (c) the speedy loss of any clear perception of the profound character of

the theological differences between them, differences which had indeed been largely responsible for their being written, at any rate in the cases of Matthew and Luke. If those factors had not operated, there is every likelihood that some of the Gospels would have been eliminated and one of them alone would have received official status. As it was, though with unequal popularity, the four came in due course to be seen as, in various ways and degrees, complementary, and, with their individuality largely suppressed, were bound together for ever in a single pair of canonical covers.

That Matthew and Luke wrote, at least in part, out of positive disapproval of Mark and other predecessors is overwhelmingly likely, and, in the case of Luke, explicit. Yet their diversity of testimony to Jesus survived, as we can now see inadvertently and by a misconception, for us to contemplate as exemplifying the theological pluriformity of first-century Christianity. We can also see that increasingly that pluriformity existed against the conscious will of many in the Church, and that, as more efficient ways of enforcement arose, especially in the fourth century, deviance was suppressed wherever possible.

All the same, with the growth of modern theological and literary perspectives, the diversity of the Gospels as theological documents reminds us of the futility of such suppression. For writings do not encounter readers as a seal encounters blank wax or print encounters blank paper: every reading elicits a fresh response, and any authority whose interest is to minimize such freshness is thus faced with toleration as a perpetual issue, just as a gardener's weeding is always an unfinished task.

In such ways as these, the New Testament may prompt us to discern some of the raw outlines of the toleration question; or rather, some aspects of it, for some of the most searing difficulties could only emerge in the more public, state-related circumstances of the post-Constantian period. It seems that at the start, the Christian gospel gave rise to some remarkable breaks with existing constraints; with Paul's style of apostleship and the sharp edge accorded to the love-command being perhaps the most striking examples. Very quickly, however, the need for clarity of identity modified these initiatives, and various groups of Christians focused their attention on self-definition over against others from whom they saw themselves as differing. Nevertheless, as modern criticism has made abundantly clear, the lack of machinery for producing uniformity, except in limited contexts, meant that pluriformity of belief and teaching was much greater than has often been recognized.

Though the matter did not *then* appear in this light, *we* may see in that situation a paradigm of the essential problem of toleration within Christianity itself. While it has only relatively recently come to be seen as a full-blown issue of both theory and practice, there has always been the problem for religious authorities, responsible for maintaining Christian identity and faced with the question of permitting or suppressing deviant or novel ideas, of deciding by what criteria to judge the matter. Quite early and almost always, those criteria have been backward-looking – tradition as exemplified in formulas of belief and the interpretation of Scripture.

With our modern sense of the inevitability of development, the task looks different: it is how to judge the direction that such inevitable change will or should take, and to enable it to emerge with minimum dislocation and without the apparatus of persecution and conflict that have in the past so regularly accompanied – but not stifled – it. Theologically, the issue now facing those who must judge whether to tolerate or to suppress is simply, what developments, in a given set of circumstances, are compatible with, even necessary for, the proper expression of Christian identity? One benefit of the relative marginalization of the churches in the West in relation to governmental and other forces which have generally, and for so long, prevented the issue appearing in such a pure form, is that they no longer muddy the waters quite so strongly; nor can they any longer be blamed for the Church's narrowness and false judgements, or for its reluctance often to view the task in such terms as I have described.

It is not difficult to be cynical about a faith which began with an act of liberation and which did indeed break down barriers in practical terms, but which speedily became intolerant and restrictive at almost every opportunity. By the yardstick of toleration, if not necessarily by the yardstick of clarity of proclamation, the Church moved from barrier-breaking to barrier-making in a very short time, and perhaps the duality was there from the start. The question of whether and in what sense freedom is inherent in Christian identity is one on which the New Testament encourages caution and heart-searching rather than yielding a single clear answer.

NOTES

1. See Peter Garnsey, 'Religious Toleration in Classical Antiquity' in W. J. Shiels, ed., *Persecution and Toleration* (Oxford, Blackwell, 1984).
2. London, SCM, 1984.
3. See Christopher Hill, *Milton and the English Revolution* (London, Faber, 1977), especially ch. 20.
4. See Ronald F. Hock, *The Social Context of Paul's Ministry*, (Minneapolis, Fortress, 1980); J. Stambaugh and D. Balch, *The Social World of the first Christians* (London, SPCK, 1986).
5. *The Letters of Pliny the Younger* (Penguin 1963), pp. 293ff.

12
In a Biblical Perspective

AIDS raises no new theological problems. All are as old as the hills, though we feel them with special keenness, as we always do in situations that are both novel and heart-breaking. Because we ourselves have never trodden a path anything like this before, it might as well be that there has never been any such path.

Different cases raise different problems. Those who find themselves HIV positive from the womb can range themselves with a Job. They can plead total innocence. They are simply victims of aberrations in the structures of secondary causes, like the victims of hurricanes and avalanches. If God lets those causes run, then no moral questions arise, though one might complain about the total system while being at a loss to imagine an alternative. A resolute Augustinian, it is true, would silence the pleas of innocence, even in cases like these: to be human after the fall is to deserve condemnation and not to be condemned is purest grace. But pitching the matter in terms of justice like this does not now win many hearts. It is a doctrine which would reduce Job himself to an even more abject silence than that brought about by God's overwhelming majesty, as in the book. But it has the merit of placing us all firmly in the same boat, which is where we belong.

In most cases of AIDS, however, the question of

deserts comes into the picture from the start; or at least it proves very hard to ignore it. Yet it is hard to bring it in satisfactorily. Leaving aside the matter of causation in the universe and supposing we limit ourselves to thinking in terms of conduct eliciting punishment, we are bound to find the situation extraordinary. The 'punishment' falls randomly, arbitrarily, and with strange concentration on a single offence; as if God were like a chief constable who goes all out for pick-pockets but leaves the burglars aburgling and the pimps apimping with impunity. The Augustinian doctrine of punishment universally deserved makes much more sense than this. It is ironic that some of those who focus on AIDS as specific punishment for specific sin show themselves less than faithful to the Augustinian tradition which has been so formative in their Protestant heritage.

The problem resolves itself into yet another dramatic instance of random, disproportionate suffering. In Judaism and Christianity the classical responses to that phenomenon are akin to each other. They are the story of the *aqedah* (Isaac's 'binding' for sacrificial death narrowly averted) and the crucifixion of Jesus. In the former case, we focus on the story of a putative event; but the aspect of it as event is dispensable, it is the story that matters and invites ever more fathoming. In the latter case, we focus on the event (this happened to Jesus), and the story serves to preserve the memory of it and to interpret it. The two are so far akin that the former is part of the interpretation of the latter from the earliest level of that interpretation. Paul uses its wording in Romans 8.32, and it leaves its mark else-where in the New Testament.

The kinship between the two episodes consists over-ridingly of a single principle. It is that significant good comes by the skin of one's teeth – and it is to be noted that the expression is derived from Job (19.20). It is of course a matter of the deepest offence, inconvenience and even outrage that this principle should be so essential to the achieving of good. One could hope for smooth progress towards that goal, a journey of gradually evolving attainment, and one can point to lives of that kind. But the good reached by that path often lacks maturity of understanding and may be underappreciated. It has been gained without going through the mill.

This principle is often referred to by Christians as that of death and resurrection, and, because of Jesus, tied specifically to Christianity. But that severs the important link with Judaism; moreoever, it is easily misunderstood when put in those terms. For it is not that resurrection follows death in the way that day follows night, simply a matter of sequence and dependability. It is rather that without death there is not a chance of resurrection; without destruction not a chance of salvation; without painful adolescence not a chance of worthwhile adulthood; without loss of innocence not a chance of sanctity (cf. John 12.24). Let us stick to the principle of good attained by the skin of one's teeth.

A man told of the worst ten weeks of his life. They were spent in mental breakdown, a time of catastrophe and constant pain, of collapse of family and framework of life. It was unmitigated evil at the time. Yet he counted this period as the source of all his good. All he had come to understand stemmed from the experience, all his selfhood, his poise and his manageable hopes. That it should be so was in no way predictable or automatic. It could not be reckoned on, and the good might never have been gained at all. It was good reached by the skin of his teeth, grace hanging by a thread – though also abundant and, once known, overwhelming and certain.

Now if this is the principle for interpreting the disastrous elements and episodes in our lives (and of course we may ignore it or find it incredible, so that disaster becomes a terminus), then it bypasses the scheme which works in terms of justice – that which might be expected of God and the deserts which we incur. On reflection, 'bypasses' is not the best word, for it suggests that the 'justice' scheme is adequate and remains in place, but we manage to steer round it, choosing a more promising route. So perhaps the effect of our principle is rather to transcend or (if that should seem too detached) to subvert and undermine the justice scheme.

It is at this point that the New Testament appears to protest. Is not Paul in particular, the earliest interpreter of Jesus' career and achievement, full of the language of justice? Yes, but he himself adopts it only to subvert it. In Jesus he discerns the one in relation to whom God 'acquits' the ungodly (Rom. 4.5), acting in a way that shatters the system of deserts as the mode of God's dealings with us. There have been interminable attempts to save Paul for the cause of God's justice in the familiar sense of his essential equity. But it is not this that concerns Paul: the language is used only to be destroyed. To acquit the guilty is to subvert justice. Such statements are followed not by sober full stops but by exclamation marks. The principle God uses is not justice, but salvation by the skin of one's teeth. How else can we understand Paul's view of the whole sweep of history: 'For God has consigned all men to disobedience, that he may have mercy upon all' (Rom. 11.32)? Justice makes no sense of that, but cries aloud in outrage. The one who has reached great good by the skin of his or her teeth knows what it means.

The principle is clear enough in the story of Isaac told in Genesis 22. Is it so clear in the story of Jesus' death? It is very clear in the first telling of that story in the Gospel of Mark. There Jesus' death is, for him, unmitigated catastrophe, as his final words (15.34) make clear (or, if they mean something else, they do not make that clear!): 'My God, my God, why hast thou forsaken me?' Almost unmitigated are the hostility and incomprehension with which Jesus is surrounded – rejected by Jewish leaders, Roman governor and his own disciples. Only certain individuals press through to gestures of faith: the woman who anoints him beforehand for his burial, Simon who carries the cross (which, in the metaphorical sense of the term, 8.34, the disciples wholly fail to do), and the centurion–executioner himself (14.3–9; 15.21, 39). They foreshadow the full flowering of good which remains obscured to the very end; for if it is too much to say that the resurrection is only hinted at in this Gospel, it is certainly not described or celebrated. To do that would run the risk of turning the cross into a wrong soon mended. Good is achieved not by natural progression but by the skin of the teeth. We are left in no doubt that there exists no other way through, neither for Jesus nor for those who are attached to him. It is the principle enjoined on his followers (in vain, 8.34; 10.35–45), and implicit in the experience of those disabled ones whom Jesus brings out of personal disaster to follow him 'in the way' (e.g. 10.46–52).

Mark gives no hint in all of this of seeing any difficulty in relation to considerations of deserts. Nobody is assessed on grounds of merit, nor is the situation as a whole interpreted along such lines. Rather, especially as far as Jesus is concerned, his story flies in the face of the structures of justice; not in order to scorn them, but in order to undermine them in favour of a different order of things, that of good reached by the skin of one's teeth.

Whether Mark intended to convey all this is uncertain; he is beyond the scope of our interrogation. It is certainly the impression he has conveyed to many of his modern readers who have allowed themselves to be gripped by the flow and the shape of his narrative. There is some evidence that he conveyed it too to some of his earliest readers. At any rate, the writers of the Gospels of Matthew and Luke, who both used Mark as their source, modified him as they used him, in such a way as to make the story of Jesus' death more comfortable at precisely the points where, in Mark, it is demanding and painful. In particular, the natural human concern for merits and demerits, for assessing responsibility and making sure it is shouldered, reasserts itself. None of us should be surprised that it was hard to preserve pure and unsullied the sense that salvation is by the skin of your teeth. It has generally remained a difficult belief to maintain, in Christianity as in ordinary life. Even those of us who are acutely aware of it in relation to ourselves, and even tell our story to others rather proudly in terms of it, scarcely preserve it when we judge other people.

So Matthew, for example, interrupts Mark's story of Jesus' death, as he, largely, reproduces it, to describe (with satisfaction?) the just end of Judas (Matt. 27.3–10). He also makes clear both Pilate's declared innocence of the sentence passed on Jesus and the Jews' acceptance of responsibility for it (27.24–5). Conversely, in 28.16–20, after the resurrection, the disciples are rehabilitated to such an extent that we almost forget their terrifying weakness only a few pages earlier. Their pain, such as it was, was but for a moment, and their future is triumphantly assured. People are morally black or white, wicked or good, chosen for condemnation or salvation. Here one has moved into a world where moral blackness and whiteness are without too much difficulty identified with colour of skin, or comparable straightforward measures of assessment. People get their deserts, and that is wholly proper. Pharisees are wholly unlike Christians.

Luke goes further in showing Jesus' disciples as

virtually 'evolving' into what is for Luke the condition of 'the good' – that of successful leadership of the mission in the name of Jesus. They reach it not without incident but with their essential virtue hardly impaired: if they fall asleep in Gethsemane, it is not callously as in Mark but 'out of grief'; if Judas betrays and Peter denies, it is because they are 'got at' by Satan (22.3, 31–4), and in the case of Peter it is but a temporary lapse. They are saved as if by having received a kind of immunity from Jesus, by virtue of his call, not by going through such depths that they are all but lost. Also, the resurrection of Jesus virtually 'evolves', in this telling of it, out of his death. Good Friday holds the promise of Easter, and we need never really worry.

In turning to the story of Jesus' death in the Gospel of John, there is ample room for uncertainty concerning his position on this matter. In a nutshell, it turns on the force to be given to the word 'flesh' in 1.14. When Jesus, the Word, 'became flesh', are we to understand an uncompromising assertion of his human reality, as the sphere wherein the heavenly one now lives, or are we to see a reference to a kind of instrument which the heavenly one uses for his purpose? In the account of his death, there are signs of the latter: it is a voluntary death, not one snatched or imposed (10.18; 13.37); it is a composed, triumphant death ('It is completed', 19.30), far from the anguish of Mark and more like the gentle piety of Luke's, 'Father, into thy hands I commend my spirit' (Luke 23.46). So for Jesus himself the element of crisis is, as it were, subsumed under the mantle of his divine status. The death was so greatly 'glorious' that the resurrection could scarcely add glory. Similarly, the prayer of chapter 17 weaves verbally a protective web around his followers: whatever evil may happen, they will certainly come through, not by the skin of their teeth, but in full armour. As for the Jews, their deep wickedness, irrevocable and incurable, emerges clearly in 8.37–59.

The key to this development in the interpretation of Jesus' death, and of the position of those involved in it, lies partly in the increasing need of the churches of the later first century to understand their own past, and elements of their contemporary scene (e.g. Jewish antagonists), in a way that was clear-cut, justificatory, and reassuring. A profound belief in the common features of humankind is an easy casualty before the pressures of such institutional considerations. 'The other' ceases to be elements within us from which we need deliverance and which we must overcome to reach that good which is only attainable by the skin of our teeth; it becomes 'the other lot', now depersonalized and generalized, those whose plain wickedness lets us off, so that we may progress smoothly towards our perfection and see ourselves as already assured of it.

All this is a great deal wider than the AIDS crisis, but there are those who have found its truth by the way of this example of devastation. It is hard to confine oneself to the essential questions, but emergencies have that effect. The underlying message of the New Testament is that the emergency is now, for us all.

Index

INDEX